8/00

The Road to Arnhem

Also by Donald R. Burgett

Currahee!

Seven Roads to Hell

The Road to Arnhem
A Screaming Eagle in Holland

Donald R. Burgett

PRESIDIO

Published by Presidio Press Inc.
505 B San Marin Drive, Suite 300
Novato, CA 94945-1340

Library of Congress Cataloging-in-Publication Data

Burgett, Donald R. (Donald Robert), 1925–
    The Road to Arnhem : a Screaming Eagle in Holland / Donald R. Burgett.
            p.   cm.
    ISBN 0-89141-682-X
    1. Burgett, Donald R. (Donald Robert), 1925–   . 2. United States. Army. Airborne Division, 101st—History. 3. United States. Army Parachute Infantry Regiment, 506th. Company A—History. 4. World War, 1939–1945—Personal narratives, American, I. Title.
D769.346 101st.B87 1999
940.54'1273—dc21   99-35435
                                                                    CIP

Printed in the United States of America

For all the mothers and wives who waited through the fearful years of World War II, one lonely hour at a time for the return of their loved ones.

Contents

Acknowledgments

My gratitude and thanks to Dr. Stephen E. Ambrose for his kind reviews and enthusiastic support of my previous works. To my wife Twyla Moonen (Mooneen) for her undying faith. My agent Rhonda J. Winchell of The Author's Agency for her tireless work and success in placing my writings. To all the members of Presidio Press, in accepting the challenge and the fine work they have produced. To Ed Benecke, a fellow 101st combat paratrooper for the many photos from his private collection that he has allowed me to use. And to Mark Bando, military historian, writer, and close friend who aided me with his knowledge of German military and his permission to use selections from his collection of World War II photos is greatly appreciated. Thank you, one and all.

1
Return to Aldbourne

I was discharged from the American 216th General Hospital in Coventry, England, on July 12, 1944, after recovering from wounds received on June 13 during the fighting in Normandy. I was a paratrooper, a proud member of the elite 101st "Screaming Eagle" Airborne Division that led the way in the D day invasion on June 6, 1944. My stick parachuted in at 1:14 A.M.—among the very first Allied troops to land on French soil that day. The seaborne landings followed us in a little over five hours later, and our infantry had to fight their way through a bloody hell on the beaches of Omaha and Utah, to link up with us farther inland on a later day.

I was issued train tickets for the trip back to Aldbourne. Rail was the main mode of travel in England. They also gave me meal tickets good for meals in any U.S. mess, and a ration card so I could purchase sundry items such as a razor, blades, toilet articles, candy, and cigarettes at any U.S. military post exchange. A clerk handed me my travel orders and cautioned me not to get caught off base without them. I also drew a small advance against my next pay. With all these papers safely tucked in an inside pocket of my jacket I made my way back to our base camp.

Traveling by English train always held a certain fascination for me. Entering one of the many side doors in a car at the station, one would find oneself in a sort of semiprivate compartment, perhaps with a few others, sitting alone or in groups of two to four on benchlike seats facing across a narrow aisle.

The English appeared to me to be a reserved people. They didn't try to invade another's privacy with questions or idle talk. They preferred to leave well enough alone and mind their own affairs. However, if engaged in talk, nearly all of them would respond in a friendly manner. At the moment I felt that I would rather be alone and managed a seat next to a window where I could mind my own business while watching the passing landscape. Looking out the window helped pass the time while in transit. You can learn a lot by watching a foreign land from a moving train, for most trains run through the backyards of the cities and the rural countryside where the common people live.

Most of the hearing had returned to my right ear, which had been damaged by a German hand grenade in a bayonet charge we made against the enemy just outside Carentan. We lost many of our comrades, both killed and wounded, and we killed so many Germans in that battle that the fields were filled with the gore-covered bodies of the dead from both armies. My right arm, which was nearly severed by a shell fragment later in that same attack, felt as though it had not healed all the way. Most of my right forearm down through my hand was still numb, tingling, sort of like when your foot goes to sleep. The wound was tender to the touch and the strength had not yet fully returned to my arm. Now I was heading back to camp and a return to full duty. Nonetheless, it would be good to get back.

Upon arriving in Aldbourne, I walked through the village square. The town was almost deserted. A few civilians turned to look at me but I didn't recognize any of them. I was the first from our outfit to return after the Normandy jump.

I walked through the camp's gateway and then stopped and stood for a long time in the courtyard. It was deserted. The rows of stables we had called home were just as we had left them when we moved out to enplane in the marshaling areas for the Normandy invasion. There was no noise, no troopers hustling about, no one doing close-order drill, no officers or noncoms chewing someone's butt, no nothing—just silence. For the first time in many months I felt a deep loneliness. Opening the door of Stable 13 was like opening the door of a tomb. Memories flooded my mind. I wondered how many men were still alive. The only thing to do was to keep busy, so I gathered up all my dirty laundry, walked to the washhouse near the latrines, and scrubbed everything clean by hand. When I finished I returned to the stable and ate some fish and chips I'd purchased earlier in town. Then I went to bed.

When I awoke the next morning, July 13, 1944, the sun was shining bright. It was a great start for a day, but I was still alone. The quietness lay like a lead blanket, thick and suffocating. Once again I wondered how my comrades were doing. How many were still alive? How many had been wounded severely? I busied myself with small chores, then lay down on my bunk for a nap. I awoke late in the afternoon to a great racket that came from the center of town. It was my outfit. The men had come back. I pulled on my ODs and boots, not taking time to lace or tie them, and ran toward the gate. Halfway across the courtyard I saw them. They came running toward me, yelling and laughing like a bunch of kids on a picnic. Phillips, Benson, Liddle, Carter, Hundley, Trotter, and many others—all of them boisterous, laughing, some with arms around each other's shoulders. They were home.

So it was that A Company, 506th Parachute Infantry Regiment (PIR), 101st Airborne Division, returned home to our base camp in Aldbourne, England.

They told me I had been reported killed in action when the grenade blew up near my face. After briefly exchanging greetings I made my way to our regimental headquarters in Littlecote Manor to report that I was still alive and stop them from sending a telegram to my parents notifying them of my death. Our command was covered in paperwork. Everyone had to be accounted for: the living, the dead, the wounded, and the missing. When I arrived they were in the process of contacting hospitals to find out who from the regiment was there and how bad each man had been wounded and just when he might return to duty, if at all. After the final tally a call would go out to the "repple-depples" (replacement depots) for enough qualified airborne replacements to take the places of those who would not return to us. The division had to be built back to its full fighting strength immediately.

Usually our command did not relax. There was no time to think, no time to brood over one's losses. We had a war to fight and win. Sharp military discipline had to be maintained, and training went on uninterrupted—ever mindful of that goal.

This time our brass allowed us time to retrieve our barracks bags, clothing, and other items and to get our barracks in shape. We worked at this all day to make sure all was clean and in order. There was no telling when we would be ordered to fall out or to stand inspection, so we had to be ready. Our barracks consisted of a series of horse stalls connected in rows, some at right angles to the others, forming one large U-shaped courtyard and one small courtyard. Each stall was large enough to accompany four men, with a double bunk on either side and a small, coal-burning stove at the center rear. There was a small window on either side of a center Dutch door that we could open one half at a time or completely, depending on the weather. Semiprivate, clean, and comfortable, those stalls were the best accommodations I ever occupied while in the military.

Our company officers stayed in the manor house near the gate, facing the large courtyard where we formed for reveille, inspections, orientations, assemblies, and other activities. Each morning, Capt. Melvin O. Davis and his entourage would make their appearance at the manor's front door after reveille and then march smartly to the front center of our group to receive the morning report. That done, we were given the command to fall out, whereupon we all ran like hell to our stables for our mess kits, then made a mad scramble for the mess hall at the far end of camp for breakfast. The slower ones found themselves at the tail end of a long company line.

After our chores were done, Phillips, Benson, Liddle, and I sat in our stable talking. We talked of many things that day and late into the night there in Stable 13, but mostly we talked of those who were dead, wounded, or still missing. All the other stables had men missing—either dead or severely wounded. Only Stable 13 had all four of its occupants—Donald B. Liddle, Leonard Benson, Harold Phillips, and me, Don Burgett—return to base after the Normandy invasion. The seriously wounded were sent stateside as soon as they were stabilized and would never rejoin us. Others of the wounded healed up in England and sooner or later would come back to the outfit as I had done, to make other missions, some to be wounded again later, or killed. Very few of us lived or stayed whole to make all the missions with the regiment.

We talked of the bayonet attack we made in the hedgerows near

Carentan on June 13. So many men had been killed or wounded there, as I was, charging into the muzzle blasts of the German 88mm guns, the blanketing explosions of mortar shells, and the heavy cross-fire of rifles and machine guns, that we came to call it "The Battle of Bloody Gulch."

We won that battle that day. I was among the many wounded who was treated and picked up by one of our medics, one of those un-armed heroes who braved the bullets, explosions, and shell fragments to tend to their comrades. Their actions saved my arm.

Immediately upon our return to camp we turned our badly damaged weapons over to ordnance for repair. An ordnance man who came to our camp with a truck-mounted mobile machine shop performed light repairs. Weapons he couldn't fix were sent off to a repair depot. We filed requisitions for replacement weapons, clothing, boots, mess kits, and whatever else was needed.

I received a new M1 rifle to replace the one I had to leave behind when I was wounded. First came the messy job of cleaning the Cosmoline from the new weapons. Then they had to be adjusted and fine tuned, making sure they were in top working order. Soon we would go to the firing range to zero our new and rebuilt weapons. In combat the first shot has to count; it has to put meat on the table. You rarely get a second chance in battle. In war there is no second place; you either win or lose.

We were issued two months' back pay with the usual formality of troopers walking down one side of a long table with the paymaster, supply officer, platoon leaders, and a Red Cross representative sitting on the opposite side. The paymaster counted out the money and passed it to the supply officer, who passed it to the man's platoon leader. Each officer verified the amount and checked to see if a trooper owed a statement of charges or other outstanding bills. Whatever was owed would be deducted on the spot as the trooper moved along from station to station to the end.

The Red Cross representative, the last man in line, asked each man for his name and serial number, then he looked it up alphabetically in the sheets of papers in front of him to see if the man had borrowed a dollar or two since his last pay. If so, the Red Cross man would deduct it and then put the money in a case he carried with him. He then counted out the balance of the trooper's money and laid it on the table. The trooper was then allowed to pick it up, re-count it aloud, and sign the pay sheet. At that point he was considered paid in full for his services to date. I, as did all the others, deeply resented having a civilian paw over, handle my money, deduct from it, and count it out to me—Red Cross, or no.

We were issued ration cards and furlough papers on July 14, and troopers shot-gunned out on their own by train or truck, heading out across the British Isles to their favorite haunts or to visit places they had heard about before the war. Many traveled to Blackpool and Edinburgh, Scotland, where an American GI was a rare sight. Others went to Bristol, Bath, and London, where they wound up drinking, chasing girls young and old, and getting into fights with whomever. If it wasn't the English, Free French, or some "leg" (non-jumper), they fought with each other. There was no animosity in these fights; it was just a way of physically bragging, showing who was the toughest. Some troopers, though, went to quiet places and did quiet things.

Most of us went in a group by truck to Swindon, where we caught a train to London. Liddle, a loner, disappeared to somewhere. Phillips seemed to have other things on his mind and headed off in another direction. So it was that Benson and I teamed up together to see the sights of London, neither of us ever having been there before. It wasn't long before we found ourselves standing in front of "Rainbow Corner" in the center of London's famed Pic-cadilly Circus.

No need to go into all that happened during the next nine days and nights. Our command was extremely generous this time, giving each of us a full seven-day furlough with two days' travel time added for going and coming. We didn't spend all of our furlough on bawdy times. We did manage a tour to Buckingham Palace, where we watched the changing of the guard, the Tower of London, the famed churches St. Peter and St. Paul, the Big Ben clock tower, and many other points of interest that I recalled reading of ever since my grade school days.

We also spent our fair share of time in pubs, including The Queen's Bazaar, which we nicknamed "The Queen's Brassiere," and many others which I can't recall—except for The American Bar, which stood kitty-corner across the great square at Piccadilly Circus from Rainbow Corner. I really don't remember what all we went through—and I'm not so sure I really want to, either.

One thing I do recall was a bunch of us catching a Red Cross lady's cat while she was hosting a dinner for us at Rainbow Corner. We tied a handkerchief to the cat like a parachute and threw it out of an upper story window to several troopers waiting in the street below to catch it before it hit the pavement.

It takes five jumps to qualify as a paratrooper, and that cat made three before the Red Cross lady saw what we were doing. Yelling something very loud she grabbed for her cat just as a trooper was getting ready to launch it out the window for its fourth jump. He pulled away from her a little too hard and wound up hurling the cat out the window into the middle of the busy street below, where it was promptly run over by a passing cab. The cat never got to make its qualifying jump and we decided not to stay for dinner after all.

When our furlough was over we made our way back to Aldbourne by train, truck, or hitchhiking—most of us sick, sober, and broke. There we resumed our chores of cleaning weapons, preparing to go to the range to zero them in, and going out on field problems. There were many new replacements in our squads and platoons that needed to be taught our way of warfare and how best to stay alive when next we went into combat.

We were just getting settled in and feeling like old home week when we received orders to pack our gear and prepare to move to a new base camp location. Why? We liked it fine where we were. We had been there ever since the division arrived in England and had come to know many of the residents of Aldbourne. We felt almost like family with some folks there. We knew we'd be going back into action again soon, so why couldn't our command leave us there until after the next operation? Those were good questions but the guys with the stars have the final say, so we packed up and moved in borrowed trucks to a large open field just south of Chisledon. It was a little closer to Swindon than was Aldbourne, but we would have felt more comfortable in our old camp. To add insult to injury, we learned our stables were going to be occupied by a company of 17th Airborne Division troopers fresh from the States. They would be sleeping in our comfortable barracks while we slept in tents.

We detrucked with our barracks bags, weapons, and gear to find great stacks of sixteen-by-sixteen-foot canvas tents waiting for us. With our officers in command we set to work laying out company streets and marking spots where each tent would be erected in neatly spaced rows. We were then assigned to work parties and began dragging bundled tents to the marked spots, raising them up, and staking them down. So it was that a tent city in an open field just south of Chisledon became our new home.

It was while we were at Chisledon that I met Siber Speer. He was a new man assigned to my squad, just arrived with a group of fresh, raw replacements. I didn't like him from the first moment I met him. Why? I don't know; I just didn't like him. Speer was shorter than I was but more ruggedly built. His nose seemed too big for his deep-lined, well-tanned face. I studied his face and finally decided that if his nose were any smaller he would be out of balance. And I thought he was homely. Later, when we were put on work details together, I liked him even less. He never wanted to goof off, sneak out of camp for a few beers, or go AWOL for a little while looking for local girls. He always did whatever chores were assigned to him. He would work his butt off just because an officer or noncom told him to do something. This didn't sit well with me. The way I saw it, it was not only every GI's right to "gold brick" (goof off) and bitch about things, it was his *duty*. Speer never did either.

We were assigned to the same tent, our bunks almost touching. This irritated me. Speer and I worked on many details together in the days to come. He was always happy-go-lucky and would greet me with a smile, a hello, and a willingness to talk or work. I figured he just wasn't wrapped tight. As an unwilling listener I learned he was from New York City and that he never saw a cow before he joined the army. He was a devout Catholic and had a girl back home that he was going to marry when the war ended. He told me about his mother, speaking of her in the most reverent terms. She was an invalid in a wheelchair. He said he was going to buy her a car after he got home and that he would drive her wherever she wanted to go.

Each month he would send money home to save for his car. The first time he did so he said, "There's a wheel!" The next month it was another wheel. My feelings toward Speer began to change. Someday, I knew, he would have that car.

Speer and I gradually became friends—in time more like brothers. I no longer saw him as being homely. He was well-built, strong, and willing and able to work all day long and then some. We were always together. We did chores together and went to town and to the movies together. We even shared a few intimate things from our personal letters with each other. I realized later that this friendship was more his doing than mine, and I have always been thankful for his tolerant and forgiving ways.

A few days after we moved into the tent city at Chisledon we loaded on civilian buses for a trip to Salisbury Plain, where we would sight in our rifles, machine guns, mortars, and bazookas on special targets on the rolling ground around Stonehenge. We did not have any equipment that we could not jump with or have brought in by glider. We therefore did not have trucks or other vehicles to take large groups of troopers on field trips or elsewhere. We had nothing more than a limited number of jeeps to tow our airborne artillery or for our medics' use. Our command had to hire English civilian buses with civilian drivers to ferry us to places where trains did not travel or it was not practical to march on foot. At times we wondered just how tight-lipped those drivers were when they drove us in convoys to areas for secret training missions, or to marshaling areas for simulated or actual takeoffs. All must have been okay, though, for we never heard of any leaks of vital information.

After our return from Stonehenge we settled down for serious training—everything from close-order drill to field problems. The division and all its units were under shakedown to acquaint the new replacements and older troopers with one another and return the division to the same clockwork-like status that made it function as an elite fighting unit. The new men blended in well and soon it was as though our division had never missed a beat. We missed our departed comrades but knew we had to carry on without them.

During the month of August 1944 we learned we had become part of the First Allied Airborne Army, or "First Triple A" as it was called, with Lt. Gen. Lewis H. Brereton in overall command. Major General Matthew B. Ridgway was chosen to command the U.S. XVIII Airborne Corps, which included the 17th, 82d, and 101st Airborne Divisions and Maj. Gen. Paul L. Williams's IX Troop Carrier Command.

The British I Airborne Corps, commanded by Lt. Gen. Frederick "Boy" Browning, included the 1st and 6th Airborne Divisions, the 52d Lowlanders (Air-transported), the RAF Troop Carrier Group, and the Polish 1st Parachute Brigade led by Maj. Gen. Stanislaw Sosabowski.

The First Allied Airborne Army came into being after the Normandy invasion when Gen. Dwight D. Eisenhower, the Allied commander, saw the true value and possibilities of airborne troops. They proved they could move quickly near and far and be used to vertically envelop key enemy positions anywhere and thus gain leverage on the battlefield. General Eisenhower met with Generals George C. Marshall, the army chief of staff, and Henry H. "Hap" Arnold, commander of the U.S. Army Air Forces, to discuss the idea of an entire airborne army and get their approval to create one. The First Allied Airborne Army was the result.

One of the first orders to come from General Brereton after a meeting with General Browning was that all future airborne operations would be conducted in broad daylight. This policy was made possible by the fact that the Allies, after long and bitter air battles, now controlled the skies and could give us the required umbrella of air cover and protection on all future jumps. There would be no more running around lost in the dark, miles from the drop zone (DZ), looking for a friend or something or someone to attack.

After our Normandy campaign, at least sixteen operations had been planned to use all or part of the First Allied Airborne Army. On two different occasions our 101st Airborne Division, along with other units, moved to airfields for hastily planned missions to outflank the Germans as they retreated through France. At one point we were to jump near Paris, at Rambouillet, to cut off Germans fleeing ahead of Lt. Gen. George S. Patton Jr.'s attacking Third Army. However, Patton's all-out dash across France quickly overran our objectives, and our mission was canceled. On August 16 we were alerted again and moved to our assigned airfields. We never went to the same fields twice in a row. When we arrived we were briefed on the jump, which was to take place the next day. Before we could make ready to jump, though, Patton's forces again overran our objectives and DZs, and the mission was scrubbed.

On August 31 we began preparing for another mission. Over the next two days we were briefed, issued ammo and invasion money, and made ready for the jump. Our parachutes would be delivered to us, as before, at the planes on the fields. Our jump would probably be a bloody affair since the enemy antiaircraft artillery would have our incoming aircraft silhouetted against the bright, daylight sky. At the last minute this operation too was canceled because of the fast-moving American ground troops. However, none of us felt cheated that we would not be taking part in this one.

On September 3 another mission popped up. It was to be a jump north of Liège to seize and hold crossings over the Meuse River the next day. Field Marshal Sir Bernard Law Montgomery, the 21st Army Group commander, scrubbed that one; he had plans of his own for our use.

We returned to our tent city south of Chisledon to take up where we left off: more training, close-order drill, caring for weapons, and listening to a flood of latrine rumors about when and where our next mission would be. Would it be a wet run after all the dry runs? We were still receiving short passes, so it was anyone's guess as to when and where we would be committed. Our passes allowed us to go as far as Swindon but no farther. The next few days went by as time usually does in the military. In addition to the usual close-order drill and field problems we had to load our own grenades with a measure of powder, a cap, and then assemble them, ready for use. We also loaded most of our belts of machine-gun ammo with a hand-powered crank, and later replaced every fifth round in the belt with a tracer. In the marshaling areas there would be plenty of the preloaded stuff for our taking.

September 14, 1944, we finally got the word. We were going in again. The word spread quickly through our ranks. We had to get ready. All personal gear was to be packed in our barracks bags, leaving out only the items we would take with us to the marshaling area and what we would actually carry in our musette bags and the large pockets of our jumpsuits when we jumped into combat. Anything left behind when we loaded on the planes would be destroyed and the refuse then taken to the divisional dump to be buried at night. We hauled our barracks bags to a pile near the Orderly Room tent, where they would be picked up by truck to be placed in safekeeping in a locked warehouse until our return.

Later that day, after we had all in readiness, we climbed aboard trucks that hauled us to Membury Field. Other regiments of the 101st Division would be taking off from Aldermaston and Ghilbolton Fields. After sixteen false alarms and three dry runs it looked as if this might be the real thing. Somehow it was different this time; we all felt that we would be going in. Our new replacements sensed our feelings and became more attentive to what we did, watching our every move so they too could do the same. We could see the questions in their faces. What's it like? How's it going to be? Is this one going to be rougher than the last one? We had been there before but we didn't have the answers. We wouldn't know until we got into it.

When we got off the trucks at Membury we were immediately assigned to tents in squad, platoon, and company order. As we headed toward the tents we heard mess call. Come and get it. We had arrived just in time to eat. We left our meager belongings on our cots, grabbed our mess kits, and headed for the large mess tents, where we enjoyed a meal of fried chicken, mashed potatoes, gravy, and vegetables. We'd had the same kind of good food before going into Normandy, plus ice cream. It was true: The Air Corps did receive better rations than did the paratroops, and they knew how to eat.

After chow we were ushered to large tents where we split into smaller groups to fit each tent and went inside to be briefed on the mission. The briefings were not as elaborate as the ones we'd had for Normandy. There were only a few maps—no sand tables, no aerial photos hanging on overhead wires—and not too much talk, just the bare facts. No practice maneuvers. This mission had been pulled together on much too short notice for all of that. All we got was a short briefing and that was it.

They told us we were going into combat again, shortly after noon on the seventeenth. We would be jumping into Holland as a part of a joint airborne-ground operation known as Market-Garden. Market was the code name for the first half of the operation, which included the First Allied Airborne Army less the 17th Airborne Division, which was newly arrived in England and not yet fully unpacked. Garden was the code name for the second half of the operation, involving the British Second Army commanded by Lt. Gen. Miles C. Dempsey.

Our briefings revealed that Operation Market-Garden was Field Marshal Montgomery's brainchild. He proposed that the entire First Allied Airborne Army be put under his direct command. The airborne would drop in Holland along a fifty-mile strip of highway running from Eindhoven to Arnhem, seizing control of key bridges, strategic military positions, and towns and cities along the way. We were to hold these positions at all cost while the British XXX Corps, under the command of Lt. Gen. Brian Horrocks, simultaneously punched through the German lines on the Dutch border and fought its way to Eindhoven. From there, XXX Corps would roll over the stretch of highway we were holding open for them to Arnhem—all within three days.

After this end run around the Siegfried Line, Field Marshal Montgomery further proposed that General Bradley's 12th Army Group be placed under his command for the big push through the Ruhr Valley and on to Berlin. There was a difference of opinion over tactics and military command arrangements between Bradley and Monty, and General Eisenhower decided on a compromise that gave Montgomery the lion's share of gas and other supplies and the go ahead for Market-Garden. That meant we were on. Montgomery also insisted that General Eisenhower order General Patton to stop his advance across Europe and hold in place until after Operation Market-Garden was successfully completed. General Patton was furious when he learned that Ike had given in to Monty, and he called Eisenhower's decision "the most momentous error of the war."

The areas around our DZs and glider landing zones (LZs) would be heavily bombed and strafed on September 16, the day before D day, and again on the seventeenth, D day, just prior to our jump. The gliders would follow us in on the same zones within minutes after our last jumper landed.

Our supporting artillery unit, the 377th Parachute Field Artillery

(PFA) Regiment, would come in by glider this time. Normandy taught a bitter lesson about parachuting at night. Each field piece had to be disassembled and, along with its ammo, required at least a dozen separate parachutes. The bundles were scattered all over Normandy—in fields, ditches, woods, and marshes. The crews had to locate each other over a wide area in the dark and then locate and drag the parts of their guns to an assembly point, at times under heavy fire. Then they had to put the pieces together and drag the gun to a battery position. It didn't work very well in Normandy. I imagine that some of the parts from those 75mm guns are still missing to this day. This time the guns would come in assembled and ready to use, along with their crews, by glider in the daylight.

The briefing went on. The British 1st Airborne Division drew the toughest job. Their mission was at the end of the road, literally. They were to seize and secure the bridge over the Neder Rijn (lower Rhine) River in the city of Arnhem. The 101st Airborne Division was originally assigned that mission, but the British had previously planned an airborne mission for that area and were better acquainted with it, so at the last minute the 101st got Eindhoven and the British 1st Airborne got Arnhem.

The newly appointed commander of the British 1st Airborne Division was Maj. Gen. Robert E. "Roy" Urquhart. He had never made a parachute jump or even taken a glider ride. Not that he wasn't willing. In fact, he all but begged to take full airborne training, including the jumps. But we all have bosses, and General Urquhart was denied the opportunity to jump. In spite of that he still managed to gain the total respect and confidence of his troops during field training. It was a real accomplishment for a "leg" (anyone not airborne qualified) in an airborne outfit.

During Operation Market's planning stages the high command agreed to allow the division commanders to plan their own missions and choose their own DZs and LZs. Generals Taylor and Gavin were shocked during the final commanders' briefing when they saw the DZs and LZs General Urquhart had settled on. Although Urquhart was well qualified as a ground combat infantry commander he was totally inexperienced in airborne tactics, which dictate that air-

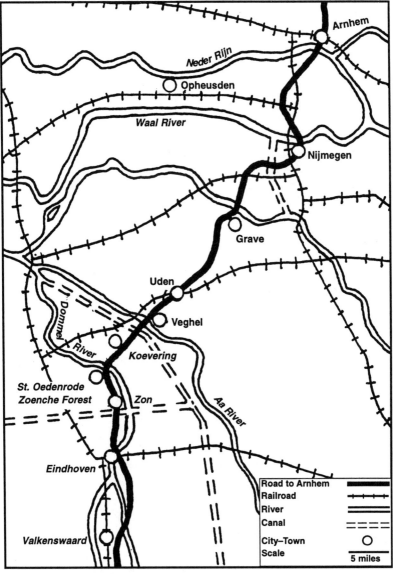

The Road to Arnhem

borne troops drop directly on or as close as possible to their target. General Urquhart, due to British pilots complaining that Arnhem was too heavily defended by enemy antiaircraft batteries and warnings of heavy losses in planes and troops if they were forced to fly within range of the German antiaircraft guns massed in and around the city, looked for alternate drop zones.

General Urquhart studied his maps and decided that the fields to the south of the bridge were too marshy for successful airborne landings. The areas to the east, north, and directly west of the city were all suitable but would have required the pilots to fly over areas where the heaviest antiaircraft fire was concentrated. To drop on the city itself, with its closely packed buildings and electrical wiring laced overhead, was also out of the question. The process of elimination led him to select several suitable areas six to eight miles west and northwest of Arnhem and his objective, the Arnhem highway bridge.

Generals Gavin and Taylor held off saying anything because they didn't want to offend the British, who had more experience in warfare. However, General Gavin later commented that he would rather sustain 10 percent casualties on an unsuitable drop zone close to his objective than land on a more suitable DZ eight miles and five hours' march away.

General Urquhart's decision meant his airborne troops would not only have to jump on their new DZs under fire, assemble under fire, and fight their way off the DZs; they would also have to fight the eight miles to their objective, ruining any chance of surprise, allowing the enemy time to fortify the city and the bridge or destroy the bridge if necessary. Finally, it meant the initial landing force would have to be divided, leaving units to stand guard on the fields and equipment stockpiled there while the rest marched out on the double for the objectives. Along the way still more troops would have to drop off to hold the road against possible enemy counterattacks aimed at cutting off the assault force from the DZs.

General Sosabowski's Polish 1st Parachute Brigade would land on D plus 2 on the south side of the Neder Rijn almost due south of the Arnhem bridge and somewhat east of the town of Elden. His mission was to reinforce the 1st Airborne Division "Red Devils" and assist them with cleanup operations and securing the bridge. He was told that if the British had not taken the bridge by the time he and his men landed, they would be expected to do the job.

Sosabowski was aggressive, resourceful, stubborn, and unforgiving. His troops would follow him wherever he went, do whatever he ordered, and he would give his life for them. He was a true leader. He had also been a tactics professor in the Polish war college. He was skeptical of the plan from the beginning—and wasn't afraid to say so. He felt the whole concept lacked proper thought, planning, and preparation. To drop airborne troops piecemeal over a period of several days, miles from their objective, and separated from their allies by a wide river was inviting disaster. To further complicate things, his brigade's supply drops would be made north of the river while he and his men would land on the south side.

To their credit, there are few warriors in the world who can surpass the Poles in combat. The Polish paratroopers didn't want to just beat the Nazis. They wanted revenge; they wanted to even the score for what had happened to their homeland and loved ones at the toe and under the heel of the Nazi boot. In spite of his misgivings, General Sosabowski and his men would carry out their orders.

The briefer explained that the Red Devils, supported by the Poles, were expected to take the Neder Rijn bridge and hold it for three days until their armored brothers in General Horrocks's XXX Corps arrived on the scene. Three days, that was all the ground units had. Any longer would spell disaster, for no lightly armed airborne unit could be expected to hold longer than that against the enemy infantry, armor, and artillery units known to be in the Arnhem area at that time. As it was, seventy-two hours would be stretching it far beyond human limits.

The 82d Airborne Division's 505th and 508th PIRs and their 376 PFA Regiment were to drop on DZs N and T east of the Groesbeek Heights. They were to capture and hold the Groesbeek Heights—which at three hundred feet in elevation was probably one of the highest points in all of Holland and commanded the flat lands in all directions for miles around—and secure their DZs for the later glider landings.

The 82d's 504th PIR was to land near and capture the eighteen-hundred-foot-long bridge over the Waal River at Nijmegen, north of Grave. It was a much larger and longer bridge than the one at Arnhem. The regiment was also expected to secure three other bridges (one of them a rail bridge) over the two-hundred-foot-wide Maas Canal.

We did not envy the 82d the task of taking the Nijmegen bridge. It was a large, long concrete and steel structure over a very wide river, guarded by an enemy willing to destroy the bridge or die for it rather than give it up. It would have been a formidable task for an army to take that bridge, let alone a parachute infantry regiment.

Our 101st Screaming Eagle Division was to land in a triangle-shaped area with the towns of Best, St. Oedenrode, and Zon at the apexes. The 501st PIR was to drop on DZ A, four miles north of Veghel, and capture and hold four rail and road bridges over the Aa River and the Willems Canal.

The 502d PIR was to land on DZ B, capture and hold a small bridge over the Dommel River north of St. Oedenrode. They were also to secure LZ W for the gliders, which would be coming in a little later than our jump and over the next two days, carrying jeeps, 75mm howitzers, 75mm shells, and all the other heavy equipment we could not land by parachute.

Our regiment, the 506th PIR, would be dropping just north of Zon on DZ C. From there we were to head south through the Zoenche Forest to take Zon, on the Wilhelmina Canal. Company A, my outfit, was assigned the mission of capturing and holding the bridge on the main road running from Eindhoven through Zon. The regiment was also expected to take and hold the two small bridges approximately fourteen hundred yards on either side of the main bridge at Zon. Once that was done, we were to proceed to Eindhoven and take and hold that city until the British armor arrived, no later than the next day, September 18.

Eindhoven was a large city of more than 130,000 inhabitants with four small bridges in it—a total of seven bridges in all for us to take. We did not know at the time we took off from England that the Germans had already blown the smaller bridges on either side of the main bridge in Zon several days before. The British high command must have known of this from the dozens of photo-reconnaissance flights flown daily over the area, but no one bothered to inform us. We were also to maintain an open road for the incoming British armor, as were all the other airborne units in the areas to the north of us. In effect we would be laying down a carpet on which the British armor and infantry was to roll freely, to, and through, Arnhem, then on to the Ruhr Valley and Germany's back door.

Major Generals Urquhart and Sosabowski had been given the most hazardous and difficult objective of Operation Market-Garden. The bridge at Arnhem was, in effect, the gateway to Germany, and every German in the area could be expected to lay down his life to keep it from falling into Allied hands.

Although Arnhem and its bridge were located at the top of the ladder extending from the Belgian border to the Neder Rijn and were the ultimate objective of the operation, the highest-priority immediate objectives were those at the bottom of the ladder, in the 101st Airborne Division's zone. The most logical place to cut a fifty-five-mile-long corridor into one's land is at its base. That was Eindhoven. If the road was cut at that point, the whole operation would fail and all the Allied paratroopers to the north would be cut off, left to their fate.

The second priority went to the Maas and Waal River bridges at Grave and Nijmegen in the 82d Airborne's zone. If the Germans could cut the road there, the British and Poles at Arnhem would face the same disastrous result.

Strangely, the last in terms of immediate tactical priority but of utmost strategic importance was Arnhem. The mission's success depended on units at each rung on the ladder doing their job. However, if the 101st Division at the base failed, all would be lost. If the Red Devils and the Poles at the top failed, only they would be lost.

Rumors began circulating shortly before D day that we had more equipment and planes than the British and perhaps some favoritism was being shown. This was partly true. We did have more planes and equipment but we also had two full divisions going in while the British had only one. As far as favoritism being shown, it simply wasn't true. The British had their style of fighting and types of weapons and we had ours. Overall, we got along famously with one another. We were always comparing things: jumpsuits, smocks, rifles, bazookas, and whatever else. One could not have asked for better comrades in arms.

We were only hours away from another D day and H hour—this time in Holland. This was no dry run. We were "goin' amongst 'em." We were "gonna stack bodies." Outside the briefing tents men came through our ranks handing out a new shoulder patch for the First Allied Airborne Army. We were to sew them on our right shoulder in place of our American flag. This didn't make sense. During our preparation for the Normandy jump and now we had been ordered, for the sake of secrecy, to remove or cover our 101st Screaming Eagle shoulder patch. Rather than remove it, most of us covered it with scraps of loosely stitched cloth. Now, we were being told to sew on the new patch and broadcast to the world that we were part of the First Allied Airborne Army. Nearly all the troopers refused the new patch or threw it away. A few men did sew them on, but *below* the American flag.

2 Operation Market

September 17, 1944. They sounded early morning reveille in the marshaling area and everyone was present or accounted for. Afterward they sounded morning chow call and we fell out on the double, grabbed our mess kits, and ran like hell to the mess tent.

The morning was cool, with a thick fog hugging the fields and runways. The air was very damp, and moisture collected on our steel helmets, dripping from the rims as we moved forward foot by foot in long lines to receive our breakfast. When I got to the serving table I could hardly believe what I saw. There was bacon, eggs—sunny side up, if you wanted them that way—potatoes, toast, jelly, orange marmalade, fruit, and coffee. We had not seen food like this since the last time we got ready to go into combat. I remember thinking it was sort of like a condemned man's last meal. Oh well, you may as well die on a full and happy stomach.

We moved through, received our servings, and found tables with enough room that we could sit together in small groups with our friends and buddies. As usual we joked about and discussed the upcoming jump with the simple air of men talking about any other job. Some talked of how they were going to carry their rifles, so as to be ready when they hit the ground. Others discussed simple things, like how and where to best carry a jump rope, pistol, knife, or hand grenades. We usually taped a couple of grenades to the upper harness with the pin wired to a D ring so we could throw it one-handed if one arm was wounded and useless. It was the usual small talk you would expect of men discussing an upcoming job.

After washing and drying our mess kits we walked back to our tents to pack our gear, then got dressed as ordered. We wore our Class A

OD uniforms under our jumpsuits. I guess the command wanted us to look nice when we had our victory parade after we won the battle. One of my buddies, George Newport, said he didn't have a clean OD shirt to wear under his jump jacket and asked if he could borrow one of mine. I happened to have one in my musette bag, so I gave it to him, adding, "I want that shirt back when this is all over."

"Sure," he replied. "I'll even wash it."

I looked out at the fog and wondered how our pilots would see to stay on the runway to take off. This worried us, but Air Corps personnel assured us the fog would burn away by 9 A.M. and we would have a warm, sunny day. It was their airstrip and their job, so I figured they should know.

Dressed in ODs and jumpsuits, we marched the long way across the mist-shrouded field in search of the C-47 assigned to us. The planes were angle parked in long, straight, shadowy lines on either side of the runway. Sergeant Ted Vetland, our platoon sergeant, carried our plane's number written on a piece of paper. There seemed to be hundreds of C-47s, although we felt sure there couldn't be that many on one field. Another large group of C-47s, each with a glider attached to it by a towrope, was gathered on either side of the runway in neat rows near the takeoff point. The gliders, filled with troops and heavy equipment and artillery, would take off after us and follow us into the DZ and LZ.

Besides our regulation weapons we carried personal weapons such as pistols, hunting knives, World War I trench knives with steel and brass knuckle dusters, and a wild assortment of other dangerous things with which to kill or maim. We also carried machine guns and tripods, 60mm mortars with bipods and base plates, bazookas, bangalore torpedoes, explosives, and ammunition.

Sergeant Vetland kept glancing at the slip of paper in his hand as we walked down the long line of planes. After a while he stopped in front of what should have been our plane but we couldn't really tell for sure because the number was scribbled on its side in a way that made it hard to read. Vetland and two others went to check out the plane on the right and found its number was one digit lower than the number on the paper he carried. The plane on the left was one digit higher. We concluded this must be our plane. We dropped our equipment on the ground and began our final packing and placing of weapons on our bodies. Several troopers began rolling up the large parapacks with the heavy stuff inside. When they finished, they fastened the parapacks to the belly of the plane, to be dropped in the center of our stick by the crew chief when we jumped.

A truck filled with parachutes pulled in close to us. We went to it, drawing at random the chute we would jump with that day.

"What's this?" a trooper exclaimed, holding his chute up in front of him by the harness.

We all lifted our chutes up and looked them over. They had a different harness than the ones we were used to. The chute was the same T-5 we had trained with and used on the Normandy jump but the harness was the kind the English used. All the ends of the harness came to the center of the chest, where they fastened to a large, single buckle. A turn of this buckle, a hit straight in with your hand, and the whole thing fell off your body. Most of us wished we'd had this setup when we jumped in Normandy: It would have saved a lot of Americans who were ruthlessly bayoneted by the enemy while they struggled to free themselves from their harness. But some troopers didn't like the idea at all.

"What if I jump and then hit that buckle by mistake?" grumbled one man. "It would all fall off and I would make one hell of a hole in the ground when I hit."

Ironically, this quick-release system was invented and patented by the U.S. Switlik Parachute Company but had not been issued to or used by Americans until now. The British were the first to use it.

Since we had never used these harnesses before and had never received any instruction on them, we had to experiment on the spot. We put the chutes on, adjusted the harness to fit, and tried and re-tried the quick-release buckle several times over. A large safety pin placed behind the buckle after all the ends were fastened ensured against accidental opening. To completely open the harness, the reserve chute's bellyband had to be opened, the fastener holding the reserve to the main harness undone, the safety pin removed, and then the buckle turned clockwise and struck straight in with the hand. This was quicker and easier than it sounds. After we jumped and our main chute opened we would unfasten the reserve and open the bellyband while we were still in the air, then pull the pin and strike the buckle as soon as we hit the ground. After trying them out a few times there on the ground we liked them.

Another truck pulled in close to our group of planes, dropping a large pile of ammunition and explosives on the ground. We were each required to carry a certain kind and amount of ammo and explosives with us to ensure we had enough for all of the platoon's weapons. Machine gunners and mortarmen could not possibly carry their heavy weapons and all the ammo needed to sustain them through several days and nights of fighting, so each man carried a couple of cans of machine-gun ammunition, at least two mortar rounds, a couple of bazooka rockets, antitank mines, TNT blocks, C-2 plastic explosive and extra fuses, Primacord, detonating caps, fragmentation grenades, and smoke grenades. In addition to this we had to don Mae West life preservers because we would be flying over water and pack a three-day supply of food, extra clothes, and personal equipment.

Near the pile of ammo was another pile of medical supplies, including an open wooden box of morphine Syrettes. We were allowed to take all we wanted because we would be landing far behind enemy lines, perhaps alone and severely wounded, and might have to care for ourselves for several days. I know of some troopers who took a goodly amount of morphine stuffed in their pockets; I took two Syrettes.

Suddenly, we were ready. Much to my surprise, the fog had disappeared unnoticed while we were getting everything in order. It was a fairly warm, sunny fall day, with little wind. I figured it should make for a nice jump if it was the same on the other side of the Channel.

We didn't have a lot of the little things we'd had for the Normandy jump. We had no metal crickets to challenge and reply with, no large, bright yellow neckerchiefs to signal with, no gas-detecting paper sleeve to wear over our right upper forearm, no gas mask, and I do not recall a challenge and a password being given out. But then this was not a night jump. We would be jumping from an altitude of one thousand to twelve hundred feet on a bright, sunny day into an open, wide, flat field in Holland at about 1:15 P.M. There was no need for all the trivialities of a night jump. We would be in constant visual contact with each other all the way to the ground and afterward. With the enemy antiaircraft and artillery positions in the jump corridor smashed by our Air Corps, this had all the makings of a true parade ground jump.

We loaded on the plane one at a time, helped up and in by members of the ground crew because all the equipment strapped to our overloaded bodies made it difficult to walk and impossible to get into the plane unassisted. Second Lieutenant William "Bill" Muir, our platoon leader and jumpmaster, and Sergeant Vetland placed us in the order they wanted us to jump in. They interspersed the new replacements in the stick among the "old men"—a title given to those of us who'd been with the unit for the Normandy jump and before. I found myself near the middle of the stick. A tall, slim, blond replacement who had transferred in from the ski troops was in front of me toward the exit door. The man behind me had arrived at Auldborne with the same group as Phillips, Benson, and I. He had made the Normandy jump with us and served in battle to the best of his ability, but now he showed signs of extreme nervousness. There was fear in his eyes; we all saw it. Sergeant Vetland placed himself behind this man so he could keep a close eye on him. The balance of the stick stretched all the way back to the cockpit door. Speer was not on board; he had been assigned to another plane.

We called the blond replacement "Ski" because his last name ended with "ski" and because he had transferred to us from the ski troops. Ski was tall for the paratroops—at least six foot two. Most of us were around five foot nine or so. John, Joe, and Bob Powers—two brothers and a first cousin—were also well over six feet tall, as was Leon Jackson. But Jackson was *big*. His fingers looked like a bunch of bananas, and his strength fit his size. Bob and Ray Teeter, a pair of identical twin brothers in our company, were small in stature. They were part of the headquarters platoon and served as Captain Davis's runners. Bob and Ray had jumped in the same stick in Normandy. Ray was seriously and permanently injured while landing. He struck the barbed wire strung from one of the hundreds of poles—called Rommel's asparagus—dotting the DZ and never returned to us.

We were all in place in bucket seats with seatbelts fastened. Two rows of troopers, seventeen in all, sat with their gear on either side of the C-47 facing each other. The men with the machine guns, mortars, and other heavy or cumbersome gear sat closest to the exit door so they could go out first. There were men in the stick to help them if they needed any assistance getting out; the rest of us would follow. The door this time, as on the Normandy jump, was in place and closed. On all our other jumps, practice or otherwise, the door was off.

This was the time I didn't like about a jump. The cabin became warm, smelled heavy of gas and oil fumes, and seemed to close in on us from all sides. We wanted to get started, to become airborne so we could get some fresh air inside. But we just sat there in silence. At last the two engines ground noisily in turn, fired, coughed, hesitated, and fired again. The pilot revved up each engine as soon as it caught, adjusted the rpms, and made sure all instruments and systems checked out. We sat with the engines running at high rpm for a while, then the pilot throttled back and we waited.

We could hear other aircraft roaring down the runway and taking off. Then it was our turn. The pilot throttled up and the C-47 shuddered and began moving. We were underway. We looked out the side ports and saw that we were in a follow-the-leader line with a lot of other planes, all heading down the taxi strip to the start end of the runway. There the planes waited a moment for the plane in front to go to full throttle and start roaring down the runway. Then the next plane in line turned left and rolled into place, went to full throttle, and started its takeoff roll. Then the next, and the next, and then it was our turn.

Our plane made the left turn, lined up with the runway, and the pilot firewalled the throttles. We gathered speed, bouncing and jouncing faster and faster—no turning back now. No one spoke; all eyes were looking forward toward the closed bulkhead door behind the cockpit, visualizing the pilot and crew doing their job. Our wheels left the ground, we climbed a little, leveled off somewhat to gain airspeed, and then we climbed out to follow the others into the sky, circling to form a vast air armada. We were on our way to a new D day in Holland. Operation Market had begun.

Upward we climbed in a slow bank to our left to join up with the rest of the troop carriers forming up over England. As it had for our

Normandy jump, the flight of aircraft grew longer and longer, like a comet circling the skies with an ever-growing tail as other planes rose from the ground to join it. The C-47s towing gliders would soon be coming skyward to form their own flight, which would follow us to the DZ and LZ, to begin landing just minutes after we hit the ground. We were part of the largest airborne invasion in history.

The British 1st Airborne Division and our 82d Airborne Division would approach their DZs from a northerly course. The aircraft carrying the 101st Airborne Division would make the approach from the south, then go west to east over our DZ. In doing so, we would be flying a long distance over enemy-held land, so flak and machine-gun fire would be heavy all the way across. Our only hope was that the Allied bombers and fighter planes had succeeded in wiping out the enemy antiaircraft batteries that were known to be in great numbers along the highway we intended to take and hold.

We were at a greater altitude than we had ever flown before as a jumping force. The air was smooth, and it remained sunny as we crossed the Channel. Looking down, I saw the white cliffs of Dover just under and to our left. I watched them as long as I could. They looked so small from where we were, and they shone bright in the sunlight. The lyrics of the popular song came to mind: "There'll be bluebirds over the white cliffs of Dover." Maybe the words of the song would come true. Maybe this invasion would make it to the heart of Germany and the war would be over. Maybe.

As our flight began to pass over enemy territory black puffs of flak appeared in the sky around us. Tracers raced upward toward us in long, fiery, snakelike paths, cutting into our planes or missing and continuing on until they burned out. We were getting hit hard and we were a long way from our target. Lieutenant Muir ordered the door removed and stored in the aft part of the ship. Our men with the heavy machine guns, mortars, and base plates fastened to their legs hooked up their static lines to the anchor cable and moved with some effort to the door opening, making all in readiness. If we were to get hit bad and have to go out, our machine guns and mortars would be with us even though we landed alone in enemy territory.

The machine gunners and mortarmen also used the new method of jumping with their weapons devised by M.Sgt. Joe Lanci of the

501st PIR's Parachute Maintenance Section. They placed their heavy weapons in a bag that was then fastened to one of their legs by a long wire that passed through connecting loops. The bag was then tethered to the parachute harness with a twenty-five-foot rope. After the trooper left the plane and his chute deployed he would pull the wire out of the connecting loops, freeing the bundle to drop to the end of the rope hanging from the seat of his harness. The heavy bundle would hit the ground first, then the trooper. The trooper could then retrieve the machine gun or mortar by simply pulling the rope to him, without exposing himself to enemy fire or having to go hunting for it, which he would have been required to do if it had been dropped with another chute.

This method differed from that used by the British in Normandy in that it was released from the leg by a pull wire. The British system was nearly the same except that the jumper had to untie his bundle and lower the bundle by hand to the full length of rope.

A forty-two-pound machine gun or mortar strapped to one leg made it awkward and cumbersome to get around on the ground or in the plane. Therefore these men always stood in the door so they could be the first ones out, even before the jumpmaster. When the time came they merely had to swing the leg with their heavy gear tied to it out the door and they were gone.

We had been flying for well over two hours. There were just a few minutes remaining before we arrived over our DZ—most of it through heavy flak and machine-gun fire. As we began our approach to our DZ the crew chief came back to talk with Lieutenant Muir and coordinate our drop and the release of the parapacks from the belly of the ship. Several of our planes had been shot down, some in flames. One exploded in midair, killing everyone aboard. We stood up and hooked up on Lieutenant Muir's order, then checked our own and each other's equipment, making sure our parachutes and harnesses were properly attached and that our static lines were properly hooked up to the anchor cable running through the cabin. One mistake could mean disaster and death. Next came the command to "Sound off for equipment check." We went through the practiced formality of sounding off loud and clear from the last man near the cockpit to the first man in the door: "Seventeen, okay!" "Sixteen, okay!" "Fifteen, okay!" And so on down to number one.

Most of us bent over slightly and watched with interest through the ports on either side of the cabin as the amount of flak in the air continued to grow. Our plane rocked and bounced with the nearby explosions. Flak and machine-gun bullets struck our plane from time to time but no one was hit. Clouds of flak filled the sky around us and tracers arched skyward in long strings while other tracers came on in corkscrew-like patterns, writhing as they searched for a victim. They struck at our flight, smashing through wings, fuselages, and the living bodies within. Others, missing their target went on until they burned away from sight. Through it all our pilots held right on course.

We clung to our static lines and the anchor cable to stay on our feet. Ski half turned to look back at me and yelled over the roar of the engines, "Is that flak?"

"Look out there," I yelled back, nodding to the port side. He bent forward and looked out the window and I did the same. The sky was peppered with black splotches of exploding shells and fiery strings of tracers lancing through the air. At that moment a large piece of the wing's surface simply disappeared. We didn't see it torn off or see or hear the impact, it just simply wasn't there anymore. In its place was a hole more than two feet wide and four feet long. We could see the ground through it.

"Let's get the hell out of this thing!" Ski yelled at the top of his voice. "Let's get out."

The line didn't move. It would be a few more minutes before we were over our appointed drop zone. We would go out on command, not before.

Our pilot held right on course throughout the flight, as had all the other pilots. They were like robots, seemingly without feeling or any sign of being excited. They held their planes at the appointed altitude and on course as we passed through the heaviest flak and machine-gun fire. When their buddies went down they still held on course. No one can ever doubt the bravery of our pilots and crews or the concern they showed for their passengers as we flew over the heart of enemy territory to our DZs. They were right on target.

The red warning light had been on for several minutes. Suddenly the green light flashed on. Lieutenant Muir shouted the command, "Go! Let's go!"

The men in the stick picked up the cry. "Let's go! Let's go! Let's get out of this damned thing." And we went. Jackson, with the 60mm mortar, was the first man out the door. He was followed closely by Carter, our machine gunner. Lieutenant Muir was next, and the rest of the stick quickly followed. In practice we had cleared a stick of seventeen men in eleven seconds. In combat it may have been faster. We had been in the air for two hours and fifty minutes since taking off in England; most of that time we were receiving heavy flak and machine-gun fire. Our flight had been losing planes throughout the entire trip.

When I reached the door I didn't have time to make the usual right turn and then left turn on exit, I just dove out headlong into space at an angle. I was aware of the ground, the sky, the ground again, and then the shock of my chute opening. Gravity took hold, swinging me down under the canopy as I began my descent. When I looked up to check the canopy bright sunlight flashed in my eyes. Still, I was able to see that my chute was fully deployed. I swiveled my head and saw the sky filled to capacity with chutes, jumpers, exploding flak, and machine-gun tracers. *My God,* I thought. I had never seen so many men in the air at one time before. I could not define my own stick from all the chutes in the air.

I glanced down and saw that many troopers were already on the ground, out of harness, and making their way off the DZ. Then I looked up and froze. A C-47 was coming straight at me. Its port engine was aflame, trailing black smoke. It was coming down right through jumpers hanging helpless in their chutes. The pilot was fighting to hold the aircraft on course. His eyes were wide and round as he was being shaken by the controls. There were possibly three figures visible in the cockpit as the plane bore down on me. I was going to be killed; I just knew it. Troopers were tumbling in haste out the door, one on top of the other, their chutes barely opening in time. I instinctively drew my feet up. The port wing passed just under me and the horizontal tail stabilizer came on, slicing through the air barely inches below my feet. I stared at the pilot as the big ship flashed by. Those moments are frozen in my memory. His gaze was riveted straight ahead. He *knew* the fate that awaited him and his crew. The plane went on, hitting several troopers lower and to the east of me, killing them with prop and wing. The plane hit the

ground, flipped up on its right wing, did a somersault, and disinte-
grated into a pile of wreckage.

The pilot had held it until all the troopers in the stick had cleared.
But it was too late for him and his crew. They all died on impact.

I stared at the wreckage for a moment, then realized the ground
was coming up fast. I had never before jumped from so high. We
were supposed to jump between 1,200 and 1,000 feet but I think we
must have been around 1,500 feet when we got the green light. It
seemed there was all the time in the world on the way down. In practice we had always gone out around 700 feet or a little less. But this
time we were high and it was broad daylight, giving us plenty of time
to look, observe, and get oriented.

I yelled at some men who were directly below me. They looked
up and moved quickly out of the way, making room for me to land.
I reached up and grabbed hold of the risers, turned my back into
the wind, relaxed, looked at the horizon, and hit. As I rolled and
got to my feet I thought about my reserve chute and the bellyband.
I hadn't prepared any of them as I had planned. Fortunately, the air
was calm. I stood there and undid everything, pulled the safety pin,
turned and hit the buckle, and was free of my harness. The first thing
I needed to do was to check my rifle. It was loaded and the safety was
on. Next, I flipped my musette bag over my head to my back and fastened it in place on my shoulder harness. Then I looked around for
someone I knew.

Phillips was about thirty feet from me. He had an equipment bundle open and was taking K rations out of it, stuffing them into his
pockets.

"What are you doing?" I asked.

"Storing up for later," he replied.

I took several of the boxes, and shoved them into already overstuffed side leg pockets and my musette bag. "We better get going,"
I said. "We've got to be with the rest of the men when we take that
bridge."

Ernest Bradison walked over to us smiling. He had a large ban-
dage on his nose. "I got the end of my nose cut off with a piece of
flak," he said. "I felt the opening shock of my chute and was doing
okay when a piece of flak whizzed by, cutting the end of my nose
off."

We asked if he was okay.

"Yeah," Bradison replied. "I needed a nose job anyway."

He had a long nose that looked a little like Bob Hope's nose. He seemed happy about it. "It'll probably make me look a lot better," he added.

Everything had gone well up until now. It was just like a parade ground jump. Somehow we had it in mind that all we had to do now was to walk to Zon, take command of the bridge, put out defensive positions, and wait for the order to march into Eindhoven.

Planes were still passing overhead and flak and tracers filled the sky. There were parachutes everywhere. Some troopers were still jumping, others were part way down, others were hitting the ground, and still others were out of their harnesses and gathering in groups before heading toward their assembly areas, which were marked by colored smoke grenades. We were a little concerned by the flak fragments falling back to earth where they could wound or kill, as well as all the equipment and men falling out of the sky. The gliders would be coming along in a minute, too. We had to get off the field.

Most of the men around us were from our company: A Company, 1st Battalion, 506th PIR. We knew them by sight, if not by name; there were so many new replacements. I looked for but didn't see Speer. A Company, with 2d Platoon leading, began walking in the general direction of Zon. Captain Davis was up front with Lts. George O. Retan and George H. Couch. Herb Erickson was picked to scout out front. We followed a two-track dirt road alongside a deep, wide ditch that had some water in the bottom. It was dry in some places and up to the knees with water in other spots. We followed the road, walking on the left side in the direction of Zon. We could see the Zoenche Forest in the not-too-far distance.

Suddenly there were shots up front. Herb Erickson had seen a German patrol up ahead. When they fired in A Company's direction, Erickson returned fire. The Germans vanished into the trees and the company moved on.

Derek "Doc" Saint, our medic, joined us in our walk. Men were headed toward the forest, coming from across the open fields as though pouring through a funnel. We looked back to watch the jumpers and someone yelled, "Look at that! Look at that!" A trooper who'd evidently had his reserve chute and harness undone to the point where all he had to do on hitting the ground was strike the large release buckle to get free of his harness had indeed hit the buckle as he left the plane. He plummeted earthward, his opened chute drifting off across the jump area with its empty harness dangling underneath. His body hit the angled top of a large haystack, glanced to the ground, and rolled. His arms and legs flailed, getting shorter as the bones broke as he rolled like a ball. He finally came to a stop some distance from the haystack.

Doc Saint stared at the man's battered body for several moments before he turned to me and said, "No sense going after that one." We continued on.

Justo Correa, John Bielski, Royce Stringfellow, Leon Jackson, Sherwood Trotter, Luke Easly, John, Joe, and Bob Powers, and several others had joined our group as we walked along beside the ditch. We came upon a lone pilot walking along the bottom of the ditch, pacing himself with our walk, at times wading through knee-deep water. He was holding a .45-caliber pistol in one hand and the steel part of a helmet above his head with the other. He didn't have a helmet liner, so he held it over his head like an umbrella. When we stopped, he stopped. When we moved forward, he moved forward. From his position in the bottom of the deep ditch he could see us but not the surrounding countryside.

"Come on up here," I said to him. "Walk up here with us."

"Not me," he replied. "I'm staying down here, that's your job up there."

Above our heads gliders filled the air. Once released from the tug ship they were committed to gravity and the earth. They came in at an average speed of ninety miles per hour so as to maintain lift and not stall out with their heavy loads. A pilot had to select a landing spot almost immediately on being released and concentrate on that spot, controlling, feeling the lift and the drop of his craft as he turned, circled, and homed in on that one spot. It wasn't as if he had power and could jockey for better position or make another pass. Once he committed his craft to land, that was it, they were going in.

Two gliders overhead and straight in front of us were banking and turning, both to their left, one a little above the other, both evidently trying to make it to the same choice landing spot. In that position it is almost impossible for the upper pilot to see the aircraft below him, and it was the same with the lower pilot. Besides, they both had their eyes glued on the target. It was the copilot's job to watch for other aircraft around them.

Both gliders were about a hundred feet off the ground. The top glider was making a shallow left turn when the lower glider banked a little more sharply to its left. Its right wing rose up and the leading edge collided with the trailing edge of the left wing of the top glider. The impact sent both gliders into violent spins to the right. It looked like it was happening in slow motion to those of us watching. The two gliders seemed to be moving so slow that we thought no one could possibly get hurt when they hit the ground. However, the impacts were terrible. The lower glider crashed straight into the ground, killing the pilot. The upper glider made about a ninety-degree turn, nosed up, stalled, and then slammed down nose first. A cloud of dust billowed up and the wings collapsed in wreckage.

We ran as a group to the site. We could see the pilot and others through the Plexiglas. They were pinned up against the front by a jeep that had broken free of its moorings and slammed forward, pressing hard against their backs. Other troopers were already breaking the Plexiglas windows with their rifle butts. We stopped to help but there were already enough men that they were getting in each other's way.

"Come on, let's go! Let's hubba-hubba one time!" one of our noncoms yelled. "There's enough help here, and we have to be at that bridge." It may have been one of the Powers brothers. I don't recall exactly who it was, but it was someone tall and slim, maybe Joe Powers. We left the wrecked glider to the men who were already busy getting the trapped crew out, and continued on our way.

Back along the ditch we came to a small wooden bridge. It was just large enough for one vehicle or farm wagon to pass over at a time. We turned left there and a short way up the road saw the remains of a bombed ambulance. It had taken a close hit of a five-hundred-pound bomb, catching fire and burning the four occupants to a char. I suspect from the closeness of the bomb strike and the condition of the wreckage that the occupants were killed instantly by the blast.

One badly charred body lay on the ground just outside the driver's door. Another burned body sat grotesquely in the front passenger seat, while two others lay outside, also badly burned. This was the work of one of the fighter-bombers that had bombed and strafed the DZ just before our arrival. The ambulance was clearly marked with red crosses on a white field on the sides and top. We couldn't understand why it had been targeted and destroyed. The only explanation we could think of was that our fighter-bomber pilots had been ordered to destroy all suspected enemy gun emplacements and all vehicles in the area.

Farther up the road troopers were turning right and funneling single file through a gateway in a barbed-wire fence. Many civilians—men, women, and children from Zon—had gathered at the gate, each eager to shake a trooper's hand or to touch them as they walked by. Two troopers stood near the gate. One of them had a camera and was getting ready to photograph our men as they passed through. As our first sergeant, Burley Sizemore, stepped through the gate carrying his personal, highly accurized, bolt-action, 30-06 Springfield rifle, the trooper with the camera took his picture

Sizemore told me in Aldbourne some time before we knew that we were going to jump in Holland that he'd had his dad send his personal rifle from home. He said he wanted to make sure he could hit an enemy at a long distance as well as up close. I told Sizemore that might be a waste. If he got wounded, as I had in Normandy, he would have to leave his weapon behind. They would not let him carry it through the aid stations or the hospitals, and he would lose his prized rifle. I told him he would be better off using an M1. It was a hell of a good rifle: semiautomatic, accurate at long distances, carried an eight-round clip, and, if he lost it, it would be replaced.

Still, he insisted on carrying his own weapon. That was how 1st Sgt. Burley Sizemore came to have his photo taken with his personal 30-06 Springfield as he passed through the farm gate to enter the Zoenche Forest.

The troopers ahead of us spread out in battle formation and began swinging left through the woods, toward Zon and the bridge over the Wilhelmina Canal.

Suddenly, without warning, explosions ripped through the trees. Men were instantly killed and wounded as dust, bark, tree limbs, and shell fragments filled the air. There was mass confusion among the troops.

"What the hell happened?" someone yelled.

"It was a booby trap," another man hollered. "Someone tripped a booby trap." "Mortars," called another.

There were more yells from farther up front. The dreaded yell. "Eighty-eights! They're firing eighty-eights at us!"

Instinctively we charged forward into the melee. We had to get to the enemy gunners and kill them in order to stop the shelling. More shells slammed into the forest around us and again dust, bark, dirt, and shell fragments filled the air. I choked on the dust and dirt as I hit the ground. There was no cover from the exploding shells and fragments. When the shells hit the trees and limbs above our heads they exploded, sending ragged, hot steel fragments tearing out in all directions, killing and maiming. There was no protection from them.

Off to my right rear Captain Davis, our company commander, lay bleeding from multiple wounds. Lieutenant Retan was dead, and Lieutenant Couch, First Sergeant Sizemore, and Sgt. Joe Powers were wounded. A medic ran over and knelt beside Captain Davis, bandaging him up as best he could. More shells struck close by, hitting the captain with more fragments. The medic had thrown his body over the captain to protect him as much as he could, and blood ran freely down the medic's left arm. He too had been hit. Captain Davis saw the blood and said, "Go on, help yourself, boy. Go work on yourself and someone else."

"No, Sir," the medic replied. "We'll get you fixed up, never mind about me."

Again shells exploded, riddling Captain Davis's entire left side and striking the medic in his left leg. I was just a few feet from them both, yet I wasn't touched. The medic kept working, taking more bandages from his pack. Captain Davis smiled slightly and said in a weak voice, "You better hurry, boy; they're gaining on you."

Men were being killed. We had to do something. Sergeant Don Brininstool, squad leader of our 2d Squad, had moved forward to the edge of the woods with our machine gunner, Paul Carter, Carter's assistant gunner, Prentice Hundley, and two ammo bearers, Earl

Borchers and Don Liddle. Carter opened up on one of the 88s that was firing at us. The gun crew evidently saw the machine gun and fired a high-velocity shell at it point-blank. Carter and Hundley were killed outright, the explosion and multiple shell fragments tearing their bodies apart. Borchers and Liddle were both severely wounded. Sergeant Brininstool received facial burns and a concussion but was somehow spared.

Shelling from the 88s and 81mm mortars heightened, tearing the Zoenche Forest and our men to shreds. All of our officers but three were killed or seriously wounded. Only Lieutenant Muir, 1st Lt. Robert E. Rutan, and 2d Lt. Anthony "Tony" Borrelli remained. Joe Powers was among the first to be wounded. Liddle, one of my barracks mates from Stable 13, had his arm nearly torn from his body by a shell fragment that ripped the underside of his forearm, passed through the elbow, and tore open a large portion of his biceps muscle. Everywhere I looked there were wounded, the bodies of our dead, and total destruction. The conscious wounded were screaming for medics but we had only three: Doc Saint, Joseph J. Molner, and Norman L. Sandifer, all of whom were doing the best they could.

Christ, I thought, *we can't just lie here and take this. We gotta go forward and end this thing.* I gathered my legs under me and dashed toward our left flank in the woods, where I could see the bulk of our men. We had to get to the enemy guns and stop the shelling. Not too far away, over toward our left flank and a little closer to Zon, I could see the back of a two-story brick building. It looked as though it might offer some protection until we could form some sort of attack. Just then more shells tore into the woods. Borchers came stumbling past me, his eyes glazed, staring straight ahead. He was mumbling, "I can't walk, I can't walk." Then he collapsed and lay there in a motionless heap, his leg bent in horrible angles, his pants soaked with blood.

Borchers survived this ordeal and returned to the outfit several months later to fight again. He had parts of a two-cell flashlight, a tin of meat from K rations, and other junk surgically removed from his legs. His leg bones were shattered. In any other war and any other outfit other than the paratroops, a man wounded like that would have been sent home. Liddle also returned to the outfit and to combat. Cases like these were more common in the paratroops than with other organizations, perhaps because of the shortage of troopers caused by our high death rate.

Running toward the brick building I hit the ground next to another trooper. A quick glance told me he was dead. His head had been cut in two by a large shell splinter that sliced through the middle of his face as cleanly as a saw. Half of his head was missing. There was a box of machine-gun ammunition fastened to the back of his cartridge belt. We needed that ammunition, so I rolled him over, undid his belt, and began sliding the ammo off. As I was doing this I saw his dog tags at the shirt opening. I looked at the name and discovered it was George Newport, the man I had loaned my shirt to just before takeoff.

More shells exploded around us. I lay flat, facedown, until the debris quit falling, then turned over on my back for a breather. There above, staring at me with one eye still intact and wide open was the other half of George Newport's head. Hanging in a tree limb. I retrieved it, put it inside his shirt, and buttoned the shirt up tight.

Shells kept coming in at a fast pace. Glass burst from the windows of the brick building, raining down in large, sharp, broken shards, to stick in the ground. I got up and ran as fast as I could, holding tightly to the box of ammo I had just retrieved. I ran until I was clear of the woods and found myself in the open facing an 88 that was firing point-blank at a group of A Company troopers who were breaking from the woods in force and running headlong across the close-cropped grass toward the 88 positions. An attack was well underway.

The bloodied remnants of A Company poured from the woods and charged madly toward the guns that had been killing us. I pulled my bayonet from its scabbard and affixed it to my rifle, then joined in, yelling and firing my rifle, charging forward as hard as I could. I saw the 88's muzzle, a burst of orange fire belching out that seemed to cover the entire scene in front of me. I felt the invisible wall of the muzzle blast as a hot, heavy concussion hitting me with terrific force. We were staggered by the explosion, but we recovered and continued to charge headlong toward the guns. *God, if I get hit, please make it quick,* I thought.

We had to get past the muzzles quick. We had to get under the barrels and into the gun pits or we'd be blown to bits by the next round fired. We kept running forward. Suddenly we were on them. We'd made it to one of the guns that had been tearing us to shreds. Several troopers went to the left of the gun and over the sandbags piled around the pit. Others I was with went to the right and up and over the sandbags on that side. A shot was fired; one of the German soldiers on the far side of the gun pit fell dead. A German soldier on my side threw his hands up over his head, turned to face me, and fell on his back against the sandbags. He was crying, sobbing like a young child. Tears ran freely down his cheeks, and he babbled over and over, *"Nein, nein, bitte. Bitte, nein."*

I swung my rifle round with the bayonet aimed at his midsection. My intent was to kill him and he knew it. Somehow I stopped. I don't know how or why, but I did. The bayonet point was just a fraction of an inch from his chest.

"Nein, nein, bitte," he blubbered again, looking straight at me.

I slowly lowered my rifle and ordered him up out of the pit. He was so shaken he couldn't rise. Two troopers grasped his arms and hauled him bodily up over the sandbags to the ground. He stood limply, his hands raised high. The troopers on the other side held three more Germans at muzzle point; they had dragged them from the gun emplacement and shoved them over to where mine stood. The Germans looked dazed and bewildered. They obviously hadn't expected us to charge straight into their muzzles as they were firing.

There was another 88 positioned to our west. Several troopers had overrun it and were crawling all over it. They too had prisoners standing in the open with their hands above their heads. There was an explosion to the east of us, toward the main road through Zon. There was a third 88 over there, and somehow it blew all to hell. Some troopers ventured that the crew had spiked the gun and then committed suicide by blowing it and themselves up. I accepted that story and believed it until years later, when I learned that a D Company trooper had crept up close to the gun along the main road and had blown it up with a bazooka.

A fourth 88 was positioned on the south side of the Wilhelmina Canal across from us, its muzzle pointing skyward. It was sitting unattended near the road next to a long building. The three 88s that had been firing point-blank at us had their barrels depressed over the sandbags to where they were horizontal with the ground. The 88 to the south of the canal was fully exposed, it had no sandbag emplacement such as the ones that we had just charged and taken. It must have been a new addition, recently arrived to help defend the bridge, and the crew had not yet had time to properly dig it in.

Evidently this 88 did not take part in shelling us in the woods. Judging by the angle of its barrel it had probably done its share of firing at our aircraft while we were coming in, but it now stood deserted. The reason it didn't fire on us in the woods may have been that it would have had to fire *between* the three 88s on the canal's north bank.

We were brought back to reality by the sounds of rifle, machine-gun, and mortar fire coming at us from across the canal. The enemy was still very much alive and present. We had to take the bridge. That meant we had to occupy *both* sides of the canal and the surrounding land.

"Let's go. Let's take the bridge," came the cry. We started as one: Benson, Correa, Jackson, Phillips, Lieutenant Muir, Bielski. All of A Company ran forward through heavy enemy small-arms fire across the grass-covered stretch of ground between the captured 88s and the bridge. German machine-gun and rifle fire cut through us. Several men were hit but we continued on.

We covered the ground quickly. Just a few yards to go and the bridge would be ours. More men were running down the main street of Zon toward the bridge. They were D Company troopers. I was staring at the bridge when it suddenly erupted in a flash of flame and black smoke. The air was shattered by one hell of an explosion and the shock wave scattered those of us who were close to it like rag dolls.

We fell prone to the ground, rolled onto our bellies, and covered our heads with our hands as debris showered the area. Some material went skyward, some of it quite large, traveling up and out of sight. Phillips was close by, lying flat and looking wide-eyed at me.

"Well, I guess we didn't get to that one in time," I said. "There's no need to hurry now. It's gone."

We lay still for a few minutes. The enemy small-arms firing had

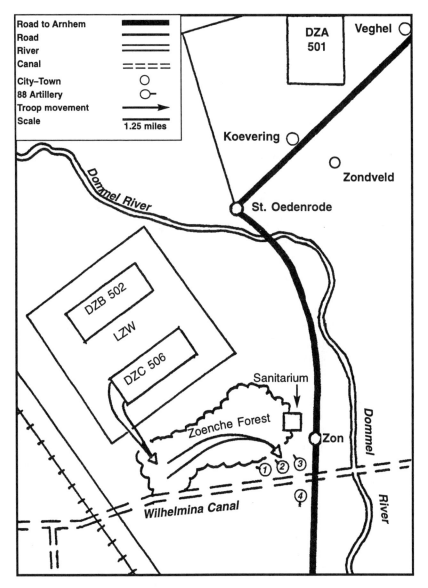

Legend:
- Road to Arnhem
- Road
- River
- Canal
- City–Town
- 88 Artillery
- Troop movement
- Scale — 1.25 miles

DZA 501

Veghel

Koevering

Zondveld

Dommel River

St. Oedenrode

DZB 502

LZW

DZC 506

Sanitarium

Zoenche Forest

Dommel River

Zon

Wilhelmina Canal

① ② ③

④

**1st Battalion Attack at Zon September 17, 1944.
Position of four 88s at bridge**

stopped; they too had taken cover at the explosion. Then we noticed a small, strawlike object floating lazily in the air, turning ever so slowly end over end, seeming to hang there.

"What the hell is it?" Phillips asked.

"Hell, I don't know. Part of the bridge, I guess."

Then it began getting larger and larger. It was coming back down. We waited and watched. Still it turned ever so slowly, seeming to drift lazily downward. Suddenly we saw the enormity of the object. My God! It was one of the main beams of the bridge, and it was coming down in our area. Without knowing which way to run, we just lay there trying to gauge where it would strike. It hit barely fifty feet from where Phillips and I lay. A shock wave jolted through the ground; we got up to investigate. The beam was made of wood and was about two feet square and maybe forty feet long. It had buried itself end first into the ground.

As we stood staring mutely at the beam I suddenly realized I no longer had the box of machine-gun ammunition with me. What had I done with it? It had to be somewhere between where I'd come out of the woods and the 88s. I recalled using both hands on my rifle when I was going to bayonet the German, so I figured I'd probably dropped it when I was slammed by the 88's muzzle blast. Someone would find it and bring it along.

Major James L. LaPrade, our battalion commander, arrived observing the scene. Without hesitating he dove into the Wilhelmina Canal and, with two others following, started swimming across. Some Germans on the other side began shooting at them. We returned fire but the Germans were well hidden in and among the houses on the south side. Major LaPrade and the two men with him gained the other side and climbed out. The enemy firing stopped. They knew we weren't about to stop here, so they made themselves scarce, fading away out of Zon.

Somebody found and commandeered a small rowboat, and a makeshift bridge made of ropes and scrap wood was soon fashioned over the canal. A few men at a time, A Company moved across the bridge to the other side to set up defensive positions. Soon the whole 1st Battalion was on hand and began crossing the rope and wood footbridge in single file. A large, hastily built wood raft with a pull rope on either end was also pressed into service. The raft could be pulled by hand from one bank to the other, carrying men or a jeep, then back again. It took a long time, but using the bridge and raft we were able to get the entire 1st Battalion and its jeeps across the canal. Our objectives were near at hand. All that was left was to liberate the city of Eindhoven and secure and hold our section of the main highway. The bridge at Zon was no more. It was now the engineers' problem.

Our company lost nearly 30 percent of its officers and men in the Zoenche Forest. Lieutenant Retan, not to be confused with Lieutenant Rutan, was among the first of our men to be killed in the woods. First Sergeant Sizemore had also been wounded and later evacuated. Just as I'd predicted, his prized Springfield rifle was left somewhere on the floor of the Zoenche Forest.

Within hours of our landing in Holland, A Company had been battered in battle and bathed in blood. One of the replacements—a young man who was always joking, laughing, and singing short Irish ballads—had said to Sergeant Brininstool as we entered the Zoenche Forest just before the 88s started their terrible blasting: "If this is combat, there's nothing to it."

A moment later the first high-velocity, flat-trajectory shell shrieked in and exploded. A fragment struck the new replacement, killing him instantly.

3 Eindhoven

Lieutenant Muir assumed command of A Company. He positioned the 1st Platoon in a perimeter around the bridgehead on the south side of the Wilhelmina Canal to defend against a possible enemy counterattack. If the enemy had hit us in force at that point we would have been in dire straits. We were dug in on the south side of the canal, our backs to the water, with no adequate way to quickly withdraw to the friendly side if need be.

Our 2d Platoon, which had been badly mauled in leading the attack through the Zoenche Forest to the bridge, now received a short respite from battle. We were now in reserve. The lone 88 still stood on silent guard near the road, its barrel pointing skyward. We looked it over curiously. Several aircraft silhouettes had been painted in white on the barrel, and several white bands had also been painted around the long barrel. I don't know the significance of the white bands but I'm sure they had a specific meaning. Our antiaircraft gunners also painted aircraft silhouettes on their guns as a record of their skill and kills.

Phillips, Correa, Bielski, Edward A. Woolf, and I walked over to the back of a long building fronting the main road and running parallel to the canal and sat in a group against the wall. Speer came walking toward us from the road, a boyish grin on his face. He had fought all the way through the Zoenche Forest as we did but we never saw each other. We may have been only a couple of feet apart at times in the battle, for all we knew. Now he sat with us, taking in the warm fall sunshine.

Sergeant Vetland soon joined us. He was getting a head count so he could adjust the size of our squads, taking into account those killed or wounded. As we sat there talking, Vetland told us about the nervous trooper in our stick who was supposed to follow me out of the plane. He said that when the trooper got to the door, the man just could not bring himself to jump. Vetland said he had suspected that might happen, so he'd placed himself behind the man instead of at the very end of the stick, as was his custom. Vetland said he tried to push the man out the door but could not get him to budge.

Precious seconds were fleeing by. Any further delay and the rest of the stick would miss the DZ and probably land in heavily populated enemy territory. The sergeant then struck the man as hard as he could alongside the head, knocking him toward the tail of the plane. As soon as the door was clear, Vetland jumped and the rest of the stick quickly followed.

The trooper who froze up was still in the C-47 when it returned to England. We heard later that he was court-martialed and sentenced to twenty-five years at hard labor. I felt bad about what happened to that man. He had volunteered for the paratroopers, passed all the training, and taken part in the Normandy invasion. He had done his best. Now, evidently, he was suffering from shell shock. Still, he tried again. He just couldn't make it. He should have been sent to a hospital and, after treatment, been put on limited service or sent home with honor and a Purple Heart for being wounded. He had done his best. Instead, he was treated as a criminal and sentenced to prison. There were a lot of deliberate draft dodgers back home who were never charged and never brought to trial. It just doesn't seem fair.

Our talk shifted to other things. While we were sitting there an older civilian came out of a side door. He tried to talk with us but neither could understand the other's language. The man smiled and made a gesture with his hands indicating that he was leaving but would be right back and that we should wait there for him. He turned and went into another part of the same building. He emerged a little later with some fresh chicken eggs and gave one to each of us. We made signs that we had no way of cooking the eggs and could not carry them without breaking them.

The old man laughed. He held up an egg in one hand and tapped a hole in one end with a fingernail, then held the egg to his mouth like he was sucking the yolk from the shell. We were doubtful, but

Phillips and I were willing to give it a try. I got a hole poked in either end with the point of my trench knife and sucked until I thought my eardrums would implode. Nothing came out. Again the man laughed. He was obviously getting a big kick out of us. I tried again, sucking even harder. Suddenly the yolk broke loose and I swallowed the whole damned thing in a single gulp. It came back up and I swallowed again. I must have swallowed that egg at least four times before it stayed down. Never again.

The old civilian then showed us the right way to do it. He broke a small hole in one end, took a straw and broke the yoke, then stirred it up. Next he broke a hole in the other end, then easily sucked the yolk from the shell. That bit of information is good to know—but only if you're *very, very* hungry and have a raw egg on hand with no way to cook it.

While we were sitting there orders came down. The 506th PIR was to move out to Eindhoven and take and hold that city of approximately 130,000 inhabitants. The 3d Battalion would lead off, followed by 2d Battalion, and then our own battered 1st Battalion in regimental reserve, bringing up the rear. The 3d Battalion formed up, put scouts out front and flank patrols out to either side, and moved out in the lead. The 2d Battalion followed at a distance with flank patrols out to the sides. Then 1st Battalion formed up and followed, with flank guards out and a rear guard posted.

Our Company, less 1st Platoon, after suffering such heavy losses in the Zoenche Forest, was held in battalion reserve and moved out between B and C Companies. C Company served as rear guard. Our 1st Platoon stayed at Zon in a protective perimeter guarding the bridge. We could not afford to lose the bridge the engineers had repaired back to the Germans, or to have the Germans move in close enough to destroy it again.

The 3d Platoon led off with our 2d Platoon following. The battalion stepped off with flank patrols and rear guard out, the men spread out in combat formation. We had gone about a mile more or less south of Zon when we came to a halt. We could hear gunfire up ahead. It lasted only a few minutes, then all became quiet again. We waited for the command to resume the march, but we were stalled alongside the road and it was getting dark. The word finally came down the line that we were going to spend the night where we were. We dug in for the night in the ditch along either side of the road.

It began raining shortly after dark and continued all night long. We didn't get much sleep. Everyone got soaked as the holes filled with water. Most of the men put their cigarettes and wallets in their helmets and kept the helmets on their heads. That was the only way to keep them dry.

The rain let up just as the sky began to lighten. We formed up again and started out. We were soaked to the skin. Our clothing was wet and soggy, and our boots made squishy sounds with each step. The plan called for us to take Zon and the bridge on D day and Eindhoven by the eighteenth, D plus 1, when the British armor was scheduled to arrive in Eindhoven and link up with us. We didn't want to be the ones to fail in the mission and cause a delay—not with our British airborne brothers in arms fighting for and holding on in the city of Arnhem. So far we were on schedule.

We munched a K ration breakfast as we walked. Men took turns carrying the machine guns, mortars, and base plates, and we all carried extra ammo of all kinds. I noticed Jackson was limping as he walked, and I asked if he had landed wrong on the drop zone and hurt himself.

"No," he replied. "I got three bullets in my right hip when we were running for that bridge back in Zon."

I told him he ought to have the medics take a look at it and see if maybe they could take the bullets out.

"Naw, I don't want to do that," he said. "I got the holes bandaged, they'll heal." He kept walking, limping as he went.

Again we heard gunshots from up ahead. The columns halted. The 3d Battalion must have run into some more die-hard Germans and gotten into another shoot-out. Within a few minutes we were moving again. That hadn't taken long. Sometime later we came to the spot where the shooting had occurred. Several dead Germans lay in the ditches on either side of the road, and more bodies were scattered in the fields to our left and right—most of them to our right. Civilians came out of their houses on the right side of the road to greet us and view the bodies. Some smiled broadly as they stood over the dead Germans.

Several of the young civilian men had taken the Germans' rifles and other weapons, including their ammo belts. They tied white handkerchiefs around each upper arm to signify they were friends and not the enemy and marched alongside us in military style, each with a German Mauser rifle over his shoulder. I looked at the body of a young German noncom lying close to the roadside as we passed. His right hand was raised as though in a Nazi salute or protest. There was a bullet hole in the middle of the palm and small, broken white bones protruded from the wound on the back side. He had a number of other wounds and was very dead—as were the other Germans scattered from the road to the handful of houses sitting a short distance from it. I figured we must be at the small town of Bokt, which showed on the map as a gathering of a few houses and nothing more. So far the 3d Battalion troopers leading the way into Eindhoven had done their work well, but Eindhoven was a big city and there were reports of large German forces concentrated there.

Again and again we heard small-arms fire from up ahead, and sometimes we could make out the sound of enemy artillery exploding near our forward troops. The Germans must have had artillery observers keeping pace with us, out of sight and out of reach, who would call for fire when they could. Each time a firefight broke out our columns would stop and we would spread out in a hasty defensive formation until the firing ceased. As soon as 3d Battalion overcame the enemy resistance we would reform on the road and resume our march toward Eindhoven, passing a few freshly killed Germans here and there along our route.

The enemy also sent small groups of troops to attack our columns from the flanks and at times head on, in attempts to impede our progress. All of these attacks were dispensed with in a matter of minutes. The enemy either left in a hurry after a brief exchange of fire or died where they stood. Since our 1st Battalion, company, and platoon were in regimental, battalion, and company reserve, we in 2d Platoon saw little action on the march into Eindhoven. We did get hit once from the right flank by a small force, but the Germans scattered as soon as we returned fire. Some of the lead A Company troopers did open fire on the enemy, but our 2d Platoon, being in reserve of the reserve, was not in position to even see a target to shoot at.

The 3d Battalion, being the lead battalion, received harassing small-arms and artillery fire sporadically every mile of the way. As the regiment's lead elements entered the outskirts of the city they were met with a barrage of small-arms fire and fire from two 88s firing point-blank down the main street. The Germans also began dropping 81mm mortar high-explosive rounds on them, effectively blocking the way and stopping 3d Battalion in its tracks. In an attempt to get a better view of the situation, Capt. John W. Kiley stepped out in the open and was shot dead by a sniper in the tower of the Woensel Church. A 3d Battalion bazookaman fired a rocket into the tower and silenced the sniper.

Colonel Robert F. Sink, commander of the 506th PIR, ordered Lt. Col. Robert L. Strayer to move his 2d Battalion east around the roadblock to attack the 88s from that direction. F Company moved south on Klooster Dreef, a road running parallel to the road the guns were on with its 2d Platoon leading. The 2d Battalion troopers then turned west on Pastorie Straat, where they encountered a Dutch civilian who offered to lead them close to where the German guns were positioned. The civilian signaled for them to halt as they approached an intersection and explained in English that one of the guns was just around the corner, across a triangular-shaped court. It was now up to the paratroopers to take care of it. The 2d Platoon's 1st squad moved up Woensel Straat, slipping through the backyards behind the houses to avoid detection. The 2d Squad went up Klooster Dreef, also moving through the backyards. The 3d Squad remained in reserve with a mortar and its crew. Two troopers armed with rifle grenade launchers led the way flanked by tommy gunners on either side.

Staff Sergeantsa John H. Taylor and a trooper named Sherwood moved forward into the cross street and saw one of the 88s about 150 yards away. Taylor fired off an entire clip from his M1 at a group of Germans rushing to man the 88. Two of the Germans fell, and Taylor's rifle jammed as he tried to reload. He and Sherwood ducked behind a building as the German crew turned the big gun in their direction and fired. The first shell went high, striking the corner of the building about twenty feet up. The Germans fired two more 88mm rounds in quick succession.

Sherwood responded by firing two rifle grenades at the 88. One of them exploded a couple of yards from the big gun. At about the same time, a 2d Squad trooper named Smith began firing rifle grenades from another position at the same target. His second round scored a direct hit on the cannon but failed to disable it altogether.

Sergeant Frank Griffin had walked forward to see firsthand just where the big gun was located. He returned to 3d Squad's location, got his mortar, and carried it back to where he could observe the 88 as he fired. He didn't waste time on the base plate; he simply held the tube between his knees as he fired. Griffin observed the strike of his first round, applied a little Kentucky windage, and fired a second round that landed directly on the gun, completing its destruction. Griffin's first round had blown a German officer standing near the 88 off his feet. The man got up and ran back toward a house. Taylor, who had gotten his M1 unjammed by this time, fired at the officer and hit him in the leg. The officer went down, got up again, and stumbled into the house. Sherwood, not to be outdone, fired a rifle grenade into the doorway through which the German officer had disappeared. The grenade's blast wounded ten more Germans who were hiding inside.

Meanwhile, 2d Squad stumbled onto the second gun and maneuvered to get into position for an attack. The crew of the big gun fired three rounds blindly at the houses where they thought the danger would be coming from. Trooper Smith fired several rifle grenades in return but scored no hits. However, the German crew became unnerved at being hammered on by rifle grenades and rifle, machine-gun, and mortar fire from such close range. Knowing the end was near, the gunners blew the breech of their gun and made a run for it. The 2d Squad fired on them and the Germans dropped to the ground as one, then surrendered when the troopers hollered at them to do so. They slowly got up and returned to where the paratroopers stood waiting for them, walking with their hands locked over their heads.

The 3d Battalion's losses included Captain Kiley, who was killed by the sniper in the church tower, and Lt. Robert Brewer, who was seriously wounded by a bullet through the throat. The Germans lost thirteen dead and forty-one captured.

That was it. Eindhoven was in American hands. In clearing out the 88s and the enemy in the northern part of the city, 2d Battalion, especially F Company, had done its work well. By 1 P.M. the road into Eindhoven was open.

As we in 1st Battalion marched forward we began to see people standing alongside the road. They waved, cheered, and threw apples to us. Food was scarce here, and for the people to give up even a few apples was a real sacrifice; it was all they could spare. We encountered more and more houses as we approached the city— houses that were built right up to the road—and more and more people. By 4:30 we were inside Eindhoven's city limits. The streets were jammed with people. Orange flags and streamers flew from every window, and here and there we saw the Netherlands flag being displayed. During the German occupation a person or family caught with an orange flag or streamer or a Dutch flag could be executed. Still, nearly every one of these people had secreted these forbidden national emblems away in their homes, waiting for this very day. Every house and building in Eindhoven flew the national flag or displayed an orange banner.

Dutch civilians—men, women, boys, and girls—greeted us with wild enthusiasm. People were smiling, laughing, waving, throwing apples, and coming into our ranks for autographs and asking for our home addresses so that they could write to us after the war. An older man who was grinning from ear to ear asked me where I was from.

"Detroit, Michigan," I replied.

"Henry Ford!" he yelled. He beamed as he told me he had put in twenty-five years at the Ford River Rouge plant and had retired and returned to Holland just before World War II broke out.

All up and down the line it was the same. People came into the streets to walk a short way with us, asking our names, where we were from, wanting our autographs and our home addresses. Every time I answered "Detroit, Michigan," some Dutch person would say, "Henry Ford." Every time the trooper in back of me would answer.

"Chicago," at least one of the civilians would hold his hands as though he was carrying a tommy gun and say, "Gangster, *Brr-rrr-rrr-ap*." So much for the influence of our American movies.

We marched on, crossing over some railroad tracks as we approached what appeared to be the center of the city. Off to our left we saw several 2d Battalion troopers herding a group of about fifty German prisoners walking with their hands finger-locked on their heads. We shouted out catcalls and yelled what few insults we knew in German at them as we walked past. I called out, *"Sie ist ein dumm Esel."* Right or wrong it was the only insult I could think of.

Our regiment's unofficial liberation of Eindhoven was accomplished before 1 P.M.—well within the timetable laid out in the original operation plan.

While F Company's fight with the 88s had been going on, the balance of 2d Battalion had maneuvered east and made straight for the four priority bridges over the Dommel River near the city's center. The 2d Battalion reached its objectives without major incident and set up defensive positions around those bridges, securing them for the British Army's use when they arrived. This was the beginning of the airborne-carpeted road to Arnhem.

Colonel Sink reported to Maj. Gen. Maxwell Taylor, our division commander, that the 506th PIR held Eindhoven and the four bridges over the Dommel River in the center of that city. It dawned on General Taylor that the 101st Airborne Division had accomplished all of its objectives ahead of time. We had completed our assigned part of Operation Market-Garden before the end of D plus 1.

That same morning our regimental communications section made radio contact with the British XXX Corps, only to learn the British were still five miles south of Eindhoven. Five miles. Battles have been won and lost in a matter of yards, let alone five miles. Montgomery's forces were held up for weeks at Caen after the Normandy landings while General Patton's Third Army tore through the French countryside chasing Germans. Five miles gave us plenty of cause for concern.

General Taylor sent a message alerting the British that the Zon bridge had been blown and for them to place a Bailey bridge at the head of their column so it would be ready to install when their convoy reached the Wilhelmina Canal. This was acknowledged and done.

By 12:30 two British armored cars scouting ahead of their main columns had skirted Eindhoven to the east, then cut back to enter the city from the north, meeting our 3d and 2d Battalions as they were fighting their way past the two 88s near the center of town. The armored cars brought word that XXX Corps was on its way with columns of armor and men. It was good news not only for the Dutch civilians but for us paratroopers as well. If the British failed in their part of the operation, the airborne troops would be left stranded on their own, strung out for miles behind enemy lines along a single highway leading into the heart of Germany.

With the British heading in from the south, 3d Battalion settled in and formed a strong defensive perimeter around the northern edge of the city. The 2d Battalion watched over the four Dommel River bridges and guarded the south side of Eindhoven. Our 1st Battalion was assigned the task of sweeping the entire city clear of any remaining Germans who might be holed up. We were ordered to bring them in as prisoners or kill them on the spot.

Our platoon broke up into small teams so that we could cover more ground in less time. Sergeant Brininstool, my squad leader, was from Jackson, Michigan. He took several men with him to search an assigned section of the city. Luke Easly, of Peoria, Illinois, the assistant squad leader, was about my height but heavier and a few years older than me. Luke took charge of the group I was with. Our group included Justo Correa, who was my size and build. Justo was a quiet, good-natured guy of Mexican descent from Carrizo Springs, Texas, and the best man to have at your side or back in combat. Then there was Speer, whom I described before; John Bielski, who was my height, broad of body, thick-fingered, and always the clown; and Harold Phillips, a blond, blue-eyed Pennsylvania Dutchman who was also a damned good man in combat. Bill Rary was a small, quiet North Carolinian. A talkative day for him was "Mornin'" in the morning, and "G'night" in the evening. But he saw and heard everything, and was very reliable. Leonard Benson, from Nashville, Tennessee, was quick-witted, dark-eyed, and an avid craps player. And there was me: Five feet nine inches tall, 140 pounds, nineteen years old, I hailed from Detroit, Michigan. We made up most of 2d Platoon's 2d Squad.

We headed toward the center of the city, crossing and following the railroad tracks that ran along the street we were on. We stayed close to the buildings on either side of the street for the protection of doorways and alleys in case we were fired on. Many buildings were damaged, and some were little more than gutted shells standing amid heaps of rubble. Up and down the side streets we went, entering buildings that looked as though they might be a good hiding place or stronghold.

Finally we came to the center of town. Here the buildings were tall, most of them office buildings. The streets were empty. Where had all the civilians gone? It was spooky, eight men walking through the war-torn, deserted downtown section of a city that was home to 130,000 people—and no one else in sight. There were no vehicles moving, no pigeons overhead, nothing. It was strangely quiet. We entered a large, tall building and began a systematic search of rooms and offices, floor by floor. We went up the stairs slowly, craning our necks to look up. It was a dangerous position. If there was anyone on the stairs and landings above they could shoot downward or drop grenades. Where do you hide from a grenade on a stairway? It would be difficult to throw one back in self-defense; it would probably clatter back down the stairs and go off at our own feet.

We finally made it to the top and went to the windows to survey the city around us. While there we discussed which of the surrounding buildings to search next, and then the next, and so on, working our way back toward the area where the rest of our regiment was.

While we were talking, Speer laughingly looked back to see if we were watching and then made a big show of pushing a button alongside the elevator door. There came an immediate rumbling, grinding noise of protest from somewhere deep within the walls. A few moments later a light came on and we all trained our weapons on the door as Speer cautiously opened it. There stood an empty elevator, awaiting our use. The electricity was still on in the city. The elevators worked. We stood there dumbfounded, looking first at each other, then at the elevator. Someone said, "Why not?" With a rush we all piled in and someone pushed the button for the first floor.

As we neared the first floor I remember thinking that it didn't seem like such a good idea after all. Anyone standing outside in the lobby could see that the elevator was coming down and would be waiting. We, on the other hand, could not see if there were any Germans waiting for us with *their* weapons at the ready. We all raised our rifles to our shoulders and waited. Finally, the door slid open. The lobby was empty. It was suddenly a good idea again.

We ran to each building in turn. If it had an elevator, we would take it to the top floor then search the building from top to bottom. We would cautiously get out on the top floor and begin our descent, room by room, office by office, floor by floor, all the way to the basement if the building had one. It was a hell of a lot easier than walking up all those stairs. Building by building we made our way back, arriving at our company command post (CP) a lot earlier than expected. Lieutenant Muir asked if we had covered all the buildings.

"Yes, Sir," said Easly. "We sure did, Sir."

"How did you clear all those buildings so fast?" Lieutenant Muir asked.

We told him that the electricity was still on—something none of us had thought of—and that we had taken the elevators to the top floor of each building and searched on the way down. He just shook his head and smiled.

We were still in reserve and, since we had cleared the downtown area so quickly, we didn't have anything to do but scout around, just looking for whatever. A few civilians had returned to the streets. Whenever GIs have nothing to do but think, the rumors begin to fly. This was no exception.

"I heard the British ran into strong German forces and won't get here until late," someone said.

Someone else said he'd heard that the Germans had moved in a powerful armored and infantry blocking force between the British and us, and that the British would not get through at all.

Despite the rumors, and even though our units continued to scour the city for hidden enemy, Eindhoven was officially declared cleared of Germans at 5 P.M. on September 18, 1944, making it the first Dutch city to be liberated.

More civilians came out into the streets. This time they offered us drinks, beer, home-cooked food, and more apples. Men and boys dressed in suits and ties, and women and girls dressed in their Sunday best wandered gaily up and down the sidewalks. Some of the girls brought flowers and talked freely to us, taking cigarettes whenever they were offered. Some put the cigarette in their purse. Others would accept a light from a trooper, take a hesitant drag on the cigarette, then cough and gag, much to our amusement.

Finally, at 6:30, British motorcycles followed by a few Sherman tanks and Bren gun carriers—the advance unit of the British Guards Armored Division—entered Eindhoven, to be greeted by an exuberant crowd. The Dutch people were beside themselves. After years of oppression, slavery, and murder, they were free. We had been waiting only a few hours for the British armor to show up and were edgy with all the latrine rumors that were floating around. The Dutch people had waited for years, and they were jubilant.

They poured into the streets in huge numbers, dressed in their best clothing, excitedly waving flags and mobbing the British vehicles, offering the occupants beer, food, and apples. The convoy soon stalled. It could not move for fear of hurting someone. The Dutch people pressed against and climbed onto tanks and other vehicles. This was their moment and they were not to be denied.

I don't know how but some of the vehicles finally began to inch forward. They were well behind schedule and had to press on. It was getting dark. The blackout was still in effect and people reluctantly returned to their homes, clearing the way for the lead elements of the armored columns to head toward Zon, a few miles to the north.

As darkness settled over the city we were ordered to form up to be marched to the center of the city. We marched confidently through the streets of Eindhoven in a loose, route-step platoon formation, not as in garrison but spread out enough so as to be combat ready at all times. We were led to a hotel and told it was where we would bivouac for the night. We had spent the previous night in water-filled holes in a rain-soaked roadside ditch; now we were being treated to plush beds in a Dutch hotel. Most of us just shed our packs and boots and slept in our jumpsuits with loaded weapons close at hand. One never knew when the Germans might come charging down on us with a vengeance again. Despite our posh surroundings we knew we had to be combat ready on a moment's notice.

The rest of the night passed without incident. We awoke early, put on our boots, hoisted our packs, and fell out into the streets. The Dutch people were already up and about. I don't think any of them really slept that night. I think they stayed awake talking, afraid to sleep for fear they would awaken and find it had all been a dream. There they were, even the small kids, thronging the streets in large numbers.

We formed up in a loose company formation. It was a small A Company since our 1st Platoon was still at Zon. But here we were, the survivors of the Zoenche Forest battle: Easly, Correa, Phillips, Speer, Bielski, Jackson, Jack Thomas, Sergeant Brininstool, Hassel Wright, Ted Vetland, our platoon sergeant, and the rest. Lieutenant Muir led us to a section of the city near the center where others of 1st Battalion were coming together on the outer edges of a large civilian gathering in front of a large building. Dutch police wearing black uniforms consisting of breeches, knee-high riding boots, and visored caps—looking too much like the Nazi SS to suit us—were escorting men and women through the building's large front door. They came out escorting other civilians whose hands were bound behind their backs and led them to where several horse-drawn carts stood nearby. The prisoners were then helped aboard the carts, which carried them off.

Phillips, Speer, Bielski, and I noted a couple of young Dutch Underground members standing close by with their armbands and carrying German rifles. We moved to them and asked what was going on.

"Those people are Nazi sympathizers," one of them replied. "They are accused of crimes against the Dutch people, even causing the arrests and murder of many of our people. They are being tried. There are many witnesses to testify against them. When they are found guilty they are taken away in one of those carts, tied to a post, and shot in the head."

While we were waiting we saw several more people being led into the building. The people in the crowd jeered and shouted out accusations as the alleged collaborators passed by on their way in. We also saw several more come out with their hands tied behind their backs. They too were escorted to the carts and driven away. The carts weren't gone long, only a few minutes. They returned empty to await another passenger. Justice was quick and final. These traitors had caused years of torment and slow death for many innocent people in Holland. At least their end was quick—if not painless.

A number of young women, some hugging a small baby or carrying a child in their arms, were taken into the street. They didn't protest while being led to the center of the large crowd but went passively. The crowd, women especially, jeered and spat at them as they were taken to a wooden kitchen chair and ordered to sit. A man armed with a large pair of scissors then slowly and methodically sheared their hair, which fell to the pavement. When he got to the point where there were only a few tufts of hair sticking out here and there he pulled out a pair of hand clippers and mowed off the tufts. Finally, he took a straight razor and shaved their heads clean, leaving them white and shiny. The women were then gathered in small groups of three to five and run out of the city with only the clothes they wore and their German babies in their arms, forbidden to return under penalty of death.

For months afterward, small bands of women could be seen roaming from village to village, begging for scraps of food and clothing. They weren't welcome anywhere in Holland.

After a while Lieutenant Muir assembled the company and led us away in a loose, battle-ready company formation. We marched through the streets to the front courtyard of a large church, where we were told we could rest but to stay close so we would be ready to move out on a moment's notice. We settled down in the cobblestone courtyard. Sergeant Vetland and a few others sat on their helmets or with their legs crossed in a row out away from the church. Most of us in 2d Squad sat with our backs leaning against the front wall near the large entrance door. Small children—boys and girls, most of the girls dressed in white smocks to keep their dresses clean— roamed through our ranks in search of sweets. We freely gave out candy, chewing gum, and other K ration delicacies.

One trooper had a camera. He had been taking photos all over the place, and now he stood to take a picture of our A Company men sitting in the courtyard. I got up and moved away from the wall.

"Come on," I said to Phillips, Correa, and Speer. "Let's get in the picture."

They said no; they were going to stay right where they were. Two other troopers joined me and the three of us went to stand behind six troopers, including Sergeant Vetland, who were sitting shoulder to shoulder on the cobblestones, and had our picture taken there in front of the church for posterity.

At 10 A.M. a column of British Shermans—along with a few Cromwells, Churchills, armored cars, Bren gun carriers, and other vehicles—pulled into the area. They pulled off alongside the road, tucking into alleys and in the shadows of buildings so they weren't lined up out in the open. Word was passed down that we would be riding on the decks of the tanks to give infantry support, acting as a screen for the tanks and to help scour the countryside for any Germans that might be left in the area. Then the order came to load up. We were going out to hunt Germans.

Several tanks with troopers aboard headed to the east of Eindhoven, out beyond the city's outskirts. The men in our squad loaded on the decks of other waiting tanks. I chose to ride on a Cromwell, which had a larger, flatter deck than the Sherman. Speer, Bielski, and I were among the several riding on the Cromwell. Phillips and the rest of our squad were on the deck of another Cromwell. We moved slowly through the streets of Eindhoven, passed through 2d Battalion's lines, crossed over the Dommel River, then rumbled out beyond the outskirts of the city.

Our patrol carried us east of the Dommel River then headed north, parallel to the main road running from Eindhoven to Zon. We gradually worked our way toward Nuenen, which was reportedly occupied by enemy troops and armor. Our job was to make sure the main road and immediate area were cleared of all Germans so the British columns could roll through unhampered, free of the threat of ambush, when the main body started out. Our British brother paratroopers far to the north in Arnhem were relying on all of us in the south to get to them on time.

We moved without incident through the countryside. We didn't see anyone, nor was there any sign of the enemy's presence. It was as though the war had suddenly stopped. After several hours of patrolling, which took us all the way to Nuenen, we failed to raise the enemy. The tankers halted in a secluded spot behind some trees and we made small fires and cooked up some K rations and coffee for lunch. We talked at some length with the British tankers, comparing our weapons and clothing to theirs. Their clothing was quite different from ours but it was very sturdy. Most of the British tankers carried American Smith and Wesson .38-caliber revolvers. About eight out of ten of their tanks were American Shermans, and they had American Willys and Ford jeeps.

"With all of this American equipment, it looks like England is going to owe us a lot of money after the war," I chided one of the tank commanders.

"Oh, no," he replied. "It's lend-lease, you know. That means you Yanks loaned all of this stuff to us for the duration. What isn't destroyed, we return. It's yours. We only have to pay for what we can't return."

That didn't sound quite right to us. Who the hell would want an old, worn-out Sherman tank after the war? Or a jeep full of bullet holes?

After lunch we saw it was fast approaching dark. Our tankers said we had better head back to Eindhoven to consolidate with the rest of our forces. We traveled back to the city without incident. A small group of officers flagged us down as we rumbled into town and told the tank commanders to turn around and take cover outside of the city. It didn't matter where, they said, just don't stay in town. It was feared the enemy was planning an air strike on the city to try and destroy the British convoy as it passed through.

Again we boarded the tanks and made our way back through the streets to the countryside. The tankers picked out a location that suited them for a defensive position. Once they had the vehicles in place the tankers not posted on guard retrieved their blankets from inside their tanks and rolled up in them, sleeping on the ground nearby. We spread out and formed an outer perimeter to better protect the tanks, dug foxholes, posted our own guard, and then settled in for the night.

It was still early when night came—and with it came the sound of German bombers. They circled above and began dropping parachute flares. The flares would ignite and hang there suspended in the darkness, casting a brilliant white light over the ground below. They sizzled loudly, like bacon frying in a pan. The flares caused Eindhoven's tall buildings to stand out starkly, surrealistic silhouettes in a totally black surrounding field.

The bombers continued to circle, dropping more flares. The city stood out in a brilliantly lit bubble in the darkest of nights as the flares floated down, sizzling and hissing like snakes. Again the bombers circled, but this time they began dropping bombs trying to destroy the British armor below. They did not care that most of their bombs were destroying buildings and the homes of civilians, killing and maiming those within.

We had climbed out of our holes and onto the decks of the tanks to get a better view of what was happening. Again and again the bombers circled, dropping bombs with each pass. The British gunners in the vehicles that were still parked in the city opened up with what antiaircraft weapons they had as searchlights probed skyward, stabbing into the inky blackness like long fingers. The lances of light moved back and forth, crisscrossing each other as they searched for the German bombers. A flare stuck in the bomb-bay door of one of the planes. The brightly lit bomber moved across the night sky. We could see it very clearly from the ground. Several British searchlights converged on the plane and held it in their bright beams of light. A large number of the antiaircraft gunners trained their weapons on the only visible target they had, hammering it without letup. Flak shells burst all around the bomber and long strings of fiery tracers lanced skyward as the aircraft fled from the scene of the carnage it had helped cause. The ground gunners fired with a vengeance. They really wanted to bring at least one of their tormentors down. So far they had not brought down a single bomber. We watched in awe as the plane kept flying through a sky filled with tracers and bursting flak. At any moment we expected to see it erupt in an orange ball of flame, or at least catch fire. Instead it continued to widen the gulf between it and the angry gunners below, the flare burning brightly beneath its belly. We watched disappointedly until it was out of sight. It never did fall.

After the last German plane left the scene and the last flare had burned out we could see fires burning in the city. There were occasional flare-ups as trucks loaded with ammunition and fuel exploded, followed moments later by the rumble of the explosions. The Germans had scored a huge, one-sided victory. They had destroyed a large part of Eindhoven, destroyed a large British supply convoy, and gotten away clean.

This same day, General Brereton, commander of the First Allied Airborne Army and General Ridgway, commander of the U.S. XVIII Airborne Corps, flew from England to Antwerp, Holland, which was still being shelled by German artillery. Together—along with their aides, bodyguards, and drivers—they took jeeps and drove from Antwerp to Eindhoven, which had been liberated by and was under full control of our 506th PIR.

On entering the city they were shocked at what they saw. The city was filled to capacity with a large British convoy of ammo trucks, fuel tanker trucks, tanks, artillery pieces, medical and food supplies, and all the necessaries with which to wage war. They weren't going anywhere; they were just sitting in place. It was becoming dark when overhead they heard then saw the German bombers arrive.

Ridgway said to Brereton, "Let's get the hell out of here." They took off heading in the direction of Zon. When the first bombs struck the generals leaped out of their jeep into a mud-filled ditch. In the dark and confusion that followed Ridgway and Brereton became separated and did not see one another until they returned to England.

General Ridgway took shelter in a ditch until dawn, then resumed his trip toward Zon by jeep with his aides, bodyguard, and driver. On the northern outskirts of Eindhoven they came upon a group of British tanks parked alongside the road. The British officer in command cautioned the group not to go any farther because of enemy forces up ahead and suggested very strongly that they take cover. The group did as advised, taking cover with the tankers.

After forty-five minutes General Ridgway became restless, then angry. There was no shooting. No flanking patrols had been sent out. No patrols had been sent straight ahead and there had been no attempt to move forward to engage the enemy. General Ridgway stood up and ordered his driver to remain with the jeep. He then gathered his entourage and walked down the center of the road past the tanks and the astonished tankers, heading north toward the 101st Division command post in Zon. The British were amazed and shocked as they sat and watched the Americans make their way down the road. About a mile north on the road General Ridgway signaled his driver and jeep forward. They all got in to continue their trip.

General Ridgway and his group made it to the 101st command post without seeing a single German or being shot at on the way. On arriving, he spoke at some length with General Taylor, the 101st's commander. Afterward the general and his group continued on toward Nijmegen for a conference with General Gavin, commander of the 82d Airborne Division.

As the darkness began to turn to gray on the morning of September 20, we again mounted the decks of the tanks and made our way slowly, cautiously back toward damaged Eindhoven. Our tanks came to a sudden stop on a small dirt road as we neared the city. Our tank commander poked his head up and told us to dismount quickly because we were receiving fire. We hit the ground running and spread outward, away from the tanks, to form a protective circle for them.

German infantry moved toward us from our right side and several of their tanks skirted toward our right in an effort to get a better shot at our tanks. We opened fire on the foot soldiers, who immediately went to ground, and the firing intensified from both sides. A couple of the German tanks fired. The shells screamed past without hitting anything and our tanks returned fire, their big guns making a hell of a blast to those of us lying on the ground nearby.

Without warning four British Typhoons and four of our Air Corps's P-47s came roaring in low, strafing and dropping their bombs on the German armor. Two Panther tanks blew up, sending black smoke skyward. Our closest tank fired again and another German vehicle blew up. We continued to fire but I couldn't see any targets to shoot at once the Germans dropped to the ground. All I could do was take careful aim and fire where I thought they would be. Some of the German infantry broke and ran back across the field, disappearing out of sight. The remaining enemy tanks roared away. The Typhoons and P-47s circled overhead and then came in low behind us. They were firing at us! Their bullets struck the ground all around us and ricochets whined away as bullets spattered against the tanks. Our men tossed out orange smoke grenades, the signal that we were friendly troops. It was a good thing the fighter-bombers were out of bombs. They broke off their strafing attack as the orange smoke billowed up, circled around again, and waggled their wings as they flew off.

We lay there for a while, waiting to see what would develop. Somebody in the enemy's area hung out a white flag. We got up and moved forward a short way and then spread out a little more and went to ground. Someone called for the Germans to come to us, which they did. We took nine prisoners, one of them wounded. We took them aboard the tanks with us and continued back toward Eindhoven again. Two Panther tanks and another armored vehicle had been destroyed. We didn't bother to see if there were dead Germans lying where we had fired on them. It really didn't matter. There had been no damage to our tanks or their crews, who had been buttoned up during the shoot-out. Nor were there any casualties among us— either from the small-arms fire or the strafing.

On entering the city, we reported as before and turned our prisoners over. Again we were told to stay with the tanks until ordered otherwise. There were reports of German soldiers and tanks in the city. Our job was to hunt them down. Much of the city had been destroyed and a number of fires were still burning. Many of the homes were turned to rubble that spilled into the streets, many of which were blocked by debris. The smoking skeletons of burned-out British vehicles were all that remained of the convoy that had been caught in the city. We felt sorry for the Dutch people who had greeted us so enthusiastically yesterday and the day before. Nearly a hundred Stuka dive-bombers, Junker 88s, and other bombers had bombed and strafed the city and the convoy for more than an hour, destroying property, homes, and vehicles. More than two hundred Dutch civilians were killed and eight hundred more were wounded or injured, many quite seriously. One young girl had her leg nearly blown off. It had to be amputated by American doctors.

All the while the German bombers had circled, dropping flares to light the area. Then they circled and recircled for more than an hour, dropping bombs with each pass. The bombers were then followed by low-flying fighters that came down to strafe. Not one Allied fighter showed up throughout the attack.

We finally found a fuel truck and our tankers topped off their vehicles and took care of whatever they had to, then they settled down for breakfast. We joined them with our K rations. After all was in readiness we climbed aboard and once again were off on a hunt. We made our way east out of the city, as before, then patrolled along a dirt road along the outskirts. The tanks stopped short and our tank commander stuck his head up and said matter-of-factly, "You blokes may want to get down for a while, we're receiving fire again."

We hit the ground and spread out in a circle around the tank. The tankers had heard bullets striking the tank from where they were inside, but we on the outside could not hear the strike of the bullets over the engine's roar. Once the tanks' engines were idling and we were away from the vehicles we could hear the sounds of machine guns and rifles firing at us from off in the distance. We returned fire in that direction but couldn't really see anyone to draw a bead on. After exchanging small-arms fire for a few minutes (the tanks never did fire any of their weapons), the shooting stopped. The enemy had withdrawn unseen, so we climbed back aboard the tanks and moved out.

We headed back into the city, our tanks moving slowly and cautiously through the streets. There were rumors that enemy armor had managed to sneak into the city and was hidden there, ready to ambush unsuspecting Allied vehicles. We hadn't seen or heard any but that doesn't mean there were none. Phillips was riding on the deck of the Cromwell just ahead of us. We were moving along a high, brick wall that someone said shielded a girls' school. Small trees lined the inside of the wall, away from the street side. We stood upright on the decks, craning our necks to see if we could see any girls on the other side, but the wall was too high.

Suddenly, a boy of about twelve came running up to us from behind, yelling. We got the attention of the tank commander, who brought the vehicle to a stop and notified the tank ahead of us to stop also. The boy breathlessly told us there was a German tank, maybe more, just ahead on the side street to our right. It was moving slowly toward the larger street we were on. Our tanks pulled up as close as they could to the brick wall and we waited.

A few minutes later the nose of a Panther tank poked out from the corner, then stopped. We could hear the tank commander in front of us talking to his gunner: "Steady . . . steady . . . steady. . . ." The enemy tank came a little farther out but stopped again. The German tank commander was being cautious. He obviously wasn't about to go charging into a blind intersection. Again we heard the lead tank commander talking to his gunner: "Steady . . . steady . . . steady. . . ."

The German tank edged out a little farther, a process that continued for about a quarter of an hour. A long time in a sudden death cat-and-mouse game. After several of these move-and-wait maneuvers—the Panther's vital parts were fully exposed about thirty feet away from the muzzle of the lead tank's main gun.

"Fire!" came the loud command. In that same instant the tank's cannon roared, belching flame. The Panther blew all to hell. A large black mushroom cloud billowed skyward. It was done.

Our attention was so intently fixed on the action to our front that we had forgotten about the young boy. I looked back but he was nowhere in sight. I had a feeling, though, that he was hiding in a safe place, watching the whole episode as it unfolded—just as we had.

Our tank commander had us dismount, then moved his vehicle forward very slowly. He eased past the tank that had done the shooting and maneuvered to the intersection, where he could get a full view of the side street. Except for the burning Panther tank, it was clear. There were no other enemy tanks. If there had been one, it must have hightailed it out of there. The tank commander had made us dismount because he knew that if an enemy tank had still been there and had fired on him, those of us riding on the deck unprotected would have been killed, along with him and his crew. He waved at us when he was sure the street was clear, and we climbed back aboard to continue our patrol.

It was late in the afternoon when we returned to our assembly area near the center of Eindhoven. There we met the rest of A Company. They'd had similar adventures with their tanks. Surprisingly, there was no loss of life or tanks.

It was one of the ironies of war. Sometimes a shell strikes and not one person is injured. The next shell comes along and half or all of the men closest to the explosion are killed or wounded. Planes have strafed a column of vehicles on the road and destroyed nearly every one of the vehicles and men in a single pass. Then the same flight hits another convoy on the same road, strafing and bombing it in the same practiced manner, and not one man is injured. So it had been when our fighter-bombers attacked the Germans and then us. We had simply lucked out.

Our squad stayed together and wandered around the perimeter in our part of the city, not straying too far from our assigned tanks. Some paratroopers were dug-in in foxholes, whereas others had found places of convenience in which to make their stand in case of an enemy counterattack.

We came across several troopers who were being entertained by young Dutch women who had brought blankets, beer, and food with them. We stopped to talk to the men and learned that the young ladies had come out just before dark the night before, carrying their blankets and food and wandering around until they found some Americans that suited their fancy. Then they had simply moved into position with the troopers for the night. Talk about luck! While we were out riding around on the decks of tanks looking for a fight, getting strafed and shot at, these men were bundled up in their foxholes with female freedom fighters.

The following morning, September 21, we awoke to the same routine. We ate a K-ration breakfast, drank ersatz coffee, and talked to a bunch of British tankers who had spent the night in our perimeter. Without seeming in too much of a hurry the tankers got ready and fired up their tanks. As soon as they were satisfied that all was in readiness, we climbed aboard and headed out on patrol again. Nothing happened all day. We saw no enemy, no strafing, no bombing, and no firefights. There was nothing to break up the monotony of riding around the countryside on the noisy deck of a steel tank. The thought of those troopers in town sharing their foxholes and breakfast with young ladies with large warm blankets didn't sit well either. We finally returned to Eindhoven and again bivouacked for the night.

Meanwhile, the men in our 1st Platoon in Zon had not only been protecting the bridge site, they helped the 326th Airborne Engineers clear away the debris from the destroyed bridge so that the new Bailey bridge could be set up without delay when it arrived with the British convoy.

The advance elements of the Guards Armored Division that had broken away from their admirers in Eindhoven moved on to Zon, arriving there at 5 P.M. on the eighteenth with the Bailey bridge. The British engineers set to work immediately on constructing the new bridge with the aid of our airborne engineers and help from A Company's 1st Platoon.

Working all through the night, they had the bridge ready by early morning on September 19. However, it was nearly two hours before the first Guards Armored Division units arrived and began sending what was to be a steady stream of tanks, jeeps, Bren gun carriers, fuel tankers, supply trucks, and all the other vehicles needed to carry the supplies of war to the front.

It was still a long way from Zon to St. Oedenrode, Koevering, Veghel, Uden, and Grave, to Nijmegen, where the 82d Airborne Division had captured the Waal River bridge intact after a heroic assault river crossing by the 504th PIR's 3d Battalion. From there it was a straight shot to Arnhem, where the British 1st Airborne Division continued to hold out on the northern side of the Neder Rijn against overwhelming odds.

At least twenty-one major and minor bridges had been involved in this operation. The Americans had captured all of their bridges intact except for the highway bridge at Zon, which was replaced within thirty-six hours of its destruction, and the bridge at Best, which was destroyed by the Germans moments before troopers from the 502d PIR could seize it. Meanwhile, the rail and main road bridges across the Neder Rijn at Arnhem were still being bitterly contested. The road bridge at Arnhem was the focal point of the entire operation: If it could be captured intact, the road to Berlin would be open.

4 Return to Zon

September 22, 1944. Our regimental CP in Eindhoven was ordered to send 1st Battalion to Zon at once. The Germans had attacked twice in an attempt to cut the road at that point and destroy the Bailey bridge that had been erected there. Somehow the Germans were infiltrating with armor from somewhere to our east and attacking Zon and the bridge. It was thought there might be a large enemy infantry and armored force in Helmond, a city a little to the south and east of Zon.

We ate breakfast and assembled in our formations before daybreak. The British tanks we had been working with had moved on. A convoy of British trucks, more tanks, Bren gun carriers, and supplies of all description was formed up on the road, facing north. The word was passed down for us to load up on trucks. We climbed aboard, then waited. A short time later the order to move out was given, and the convoy began covering the few short miles to Zon, where our 1st Platoon was still guarding the bridge they'd helped build.

We got off in Zon and the convoy continued northward. First Lieutenant William "Bill" Kennedy had been assigned as our new company commander and Lieutenant Muir resumed command of our platoon. Lieutenant Borrelli remained in command of 3d Platoon, and Lieutenant Rutan took command of 1st Platoon.

Men from all three platoons greeted one another as long lost brothers, each telling stories of what had happened since we'd last seen one another. We told of our triumphant march into Eindhoven, how we'd cleared the tall buildings with the aid of elevators, of our patrols around the outskirts of the city and along the roads from Eindhoven to Nuenen on British tanks, of the enemy tanks that had been destroyed, of the "friendly" strafing of our tanks, and of the bombing of the city of Eindhoven by the Germans.

The men of the 1st Platoon told us about how they'd had to stand guard and help clear away the debris of the old bridge, and of how they'd assisted in the building of the new Bailey bridge. Then, with the bridge in place and British XXX Corps units rolling northward, the Germans launched an attack late in the afternoon on the nineteenth in an attempt to destroy the Zon bridge and take possession of the area to halt further supply of the Allied troops to the north.

It all started at about 5 P.M. when a couple of Dutch civilians bicycled into 1st Platoon's area. They gasped for breath as they told of some German tanks they had seen in the area heading in the direction of the bridge.

Lieutenant Colonel Ned D. Moore, 1st Lt. Fred Starrett of the 101st Division's field artillery, and a Dutch army officer named Lieutenant Dubois headed east on foot along the canal to find out if there were indeed any German tanks in the area. They were accompanied by a 1st Platoon bazooka team consisting of Cpl. Jerry Janes, Pvt. John McCarthy, and Jim "Slick" Hoenscheidt, who volunteered to go along as a backup rifleman. They hadn't gone far when a camouflaged Panther tank burst from the bushes and trees about three hundred yards to their front, firing its machine guns. Two more Panther tanks followed a short distance behind with infantry spread out to their flanks and rear. The Germans were attacking along the south side of the Wilhelmina Canal headed in the direction of Zon and the bridge.

First Lieutenant Rodney Adams and a group of troopers who were in the defensive perimeter alongside the canal jumped into the water to swim to the north shore. Lieutenant Adams didn't make it; he drowned in the attempt. Second Lieutenant James Diel, who had received a battlefield commission in Normandy and had taken command of 1st Platoon, was standing with a group of his men and said loud enough for all to hear, "This is where I get the Medal of Honor."

Lieutenant Diel was always playing with explosives. He carried about twenty pounds of composition C-2 in his musette bag, several blocks of TNT in his large jump pants pockets, Primacord wrapped around one shoulder, and various types of fuse wrapped around the other shoulder. He also carried pull-type igniters and small wooden boxes of blasting caps in his pants pockets. I can recall hearing him constantly boasting that he was going to get the Medal of Honor in this campaign, one way or the other.

On seeing the enemy tank approaching with its machine guns blazing, Lieutenant Diel began packing composition C-2 together in his hands, capped a cut length of fuse, and was putting an igniter in place on the fuse while running toward the big tank. It was a very brave act—or a very foolish one. The tank's big gun fired, sending a 75mm shell slamming into an English truck on the bridge. It destroyed the truck, setting it afire and blocking the bridge to traffic. A second round hit the bridge itself, doing some damage there. A third round destroyed another truck just south of the bridge. Yet another 75mm shell from the tank struck a church steeple, probably in an attempt to get rid of any observers that might have been posted there. The turret swiveled, the gunner adjusted his aim, and a fifth round struck Lieutenant Diel as he ran toward the tank, taking his head off at the shoulders. The Panther was on a shooting rampage, hell bent on cutting the road through Zon. The men of 1st Platoon withdrew quickly to safety between and behind several nearby houses.

Lieutenant Colonel Moore, Jerry Janes, and John McCarthy slid into a hole near the edge of the road that ran alongside the canal. With McCarthy firing and Janes loading the bazooka, they managed to fire three rockets at the tank. Two missed, and the third struck the hull without causing any apparent damage. The tank commander, possibly being prudent, stopped the tank until he knew what lay ahead and how to deal with it. Others in the American scouting party that were a little farther behind pulled back on the double to the safety of the houses. Slick Hoenscheidt looked around and realized he was alone in front of the tank. The bazooka team was in a hole at the side of the road, the engineers had swum to the north side of the canal, and the rest of the men had hastily retired to positions shielded by the houses of Zon.

The flanking enemy infantry began firing their machine guns and rifles at Slick and toward the rest of the 1st Platoon scattered among the houses near the bridge. They all returned the fire. The Germans quickly went to ground. Slick, alone out front, was caught in a deadly cross fire between the enemy and his 1st Platoon comrades. Realizing he was in a precarious position, Slick jumped behind what he called "a big mushroom" on the canal's edge. Being from Kansas, he didn't know that the large wooden mushroom that shielded him was a mooring post used for tying canal barges to the shore. All Slick knew was that it offered the only cover around. He returned fire at the enemy flankers with his M1, forcing the German infantry to hit the dirt. A wounded American engineer called to Slick from the water, asking if he could help.

"Stay where you are," Slick replied. "I'll probably be with you before long."

As the Panther started to slowly advance it was struck in the right side by a 57mm antitank shell fired from the north side of the canal, again without much damage. The tank commander opened his hatch so he could look around and see where the antitank gun was located. He stuck his head out, saw Slick behind the mooring post a few yards away, and dropped back down into the tank. Seeing an opportunity to knock out the tank, Slick leaped forward, chucked a grenade into the open hatch, and dove under the tank for protection from the German machine gun that had opened up on him again. When the tank crew saw the grenade, they bailed out of the vehicle. At almost the same moment, two more 57mm shells slammed into the tank in quick succession. None of the crewmen appeared to be hit as they raced back in the direction from which they had just come. Meanwhile, a big German infantryman came running forward, probably in an attempt to get into position to shoot Slick where he lay under the tank. However, Slick shot first. The big German let out a yell and either fell or dove into the canal, disappearing from sight.

Slick was in a bad position. Alone out front, caught between a squad of Germans that was firing at him while his comrades behind him at the bridge were shooting over and around him at the attacking Germans, he was caught in a deadly cross fire. Slick reached in his pocket for another grenade but discovered he had thrown his last one into the hatch of the tank. Then he felt an apple. The Dutch people had been throwing them to and at us ever since we'd landed, and we all had apples in our pockets. He raised his hands in an exaggerated way so the enemy would be sure to see what he was doing, pulled the stem, and threw the apple at the Germans, who immediately dove face first into the dirt and covered their heads with their hands. While they were waiting for the "grenade" to go off in their midst, Slick jumped up and ran like hell back toward the Zon bridge. Some of the enemy regained their senses when there was no explosion and fired at Slick, who by that time had covered some distance. He made it safely to the shelter of the houses—out of grenades, out of ammo for his rifle, and out of apples.

The two Panthers that had remained at a distance while all the shooting was going on pulled back along with their infantry into the tree line to the east. Chalk up one Panther tank to the credit of Jim "Slick" Hoenscheidt. After the battle, others claimed credit for killing the German tank. The crew of the 57mm gun that had fired on it from across the canal knew in their own minds that they had finished off the tank. They were unable to see Slick on the south side, and what with their shells hitting at the same time the grenade exploded, they had every right to believe it was they who had destroyed the tank. Others thought that General Taylor, who had raced back to the DZ in his jeep and brought back the 57mm antitank gun and its crew, was instrumental in the destruction of the marauding tank. But all who saw him were convinced that Slick Hoenscheidt's actions were what actually brought about the marauding tank's end and caused the other two tanks and the infantry to withdraw. Slick's actions probably saved the bridge at Zon from being destroyed a second time and cutting the Allies' only lifeline to the north.

An officer who had witnessed firsthand all that transpired recommended Slick for the Silver Star. The men of 1st Platoon, and the officers and men of the engineer unit and others guarding the bridge at Zon also saw what happened. However, for whatever reason, a field grade officer who was the senior officer on the scene would not sign off on the recommendation. Denied official military recognition for his actions at Zon, I hope that my retelling of this incident here will help gain for Jim Hoenscheidt some measure of the credit he deserves for destroying that enemy tank and thereby saving the bridge at Zon.

During this engagement six Germans were killed and one wounded. Our casualties were two killed (Lieutenants Diel and Adams) and two wounded. Sergeant Sam Sutherland took command of 1st Platoon until Lieutenant Rutan replaced him.

The next morning, September 20, the Germans launched another tank and infantry attack out of the gray morning mists from the southeast, headed for the Dommel River, driving at an angle toward Zon and its bridge. This time 1st Platoon—reinforced with more paratroopers, glidermen, British tanks, and volunteer glider pilots—was ready. The firefight didn't last long, and the Germans pulled back after losing one Tiger tank destroyed, a couple of Panthers damaged, and many German infantrymen killed and wounded without getting nearly as close to the bridge as they had the day before. One trooper was killed and several were wounded.

On September 22, with Lt. Bill Kennedy in command, A Company took up defensive positions between B and C Companies in the defense of Zon and its all-important bridge over the Wilhelmina Canal.

Our 2d Squad walked a ways out on the perimeter where two men at a time were dropped off at strategic spots to stand guard. We moved up a two-track dirt road to an outer section of the perimeter. Bielski and I, with a .30-caliber machine gun and several boxes of ammo, were left to defend this area. In the event of an attack, this road seemed one of the most likely spots for the enemy to try. That's why Bielski and I had the squad's machine gun. I figured that if it were that important we ought to at least have had a bazooka team with us, but all the bazooka teams were pulled into the tight defensive perimeter around the bridge itself.

Bielski and I dug foxholes, set the gun up in a strategic spot, and then lay out on the ground in the mild fall weather. While we were lying there, three young children—two boys and a girl—came over to visit us. They spoke English and asked our ages, where we were from, and many other questions. Bielski and I gave them gum, candy, and other things from our K rations, but no cigarettes. Then we told them they would have to leave. We were worried that they might distract us with all their talk, allowing the enemy to sneak in close enough to kill us or take us prisoner. We learned from the children that studying English was compulsory in all of their grade schools. If we needed an interpreter, all we had to do was get ahold of any kid around twelve years old, because they all spoke English.

A few minutes after the children left, a middle-aged civilian couple—I assume they were husband and wife—approached us with a plate of meat, vegetables, and bread and insisted that we eat. We did not want to take their food; we knew it was scarce and what a big sacrifice they were making to show their appreciation for our being there. Finally, at their continued insistence, we ate. Then we gave them some K rations in return. They thanked us and left. Just after dark one of our men came up the road and told us to return to our company area, where we dug in with the others in close defense of the bridge.

Night passes slowly in a foxhole. You sit there staring into the dark, listening to nerve-wracking sounds like the crack of a twig, the wind in the trees, or a dog barking in the distance. At times your mind tells you you're hearing the footfalls of an approaching enemy, the sound of troops infiltrating, or tanks moving in the distance. It is always a relief when daylight appears. There is a time, though, when the sky first begins to lighten ever so slightly, that most attacks begin. That is the time when every eye and ear in the company is tuned in, when every man is fully alert.

Going back to the day we jumped into Holland, an important sequence of events happened on D day that led to a bloody confrontation. We in the 506th PIR had been busy with our assigned missions, accomplishing them all in the required time. Now we rested as we stayed on line, catching up on some of the things that had happened to the others—not only in our regiment but in the rest of the 101st Division.

Before D day, General Taylor, on examining the original plan, saw there was no provision for an alternate route from Eindhoven to Arnhem anywhere along the fifty-mile corridor. If for some reason the road was made impassable either by destroyed bridges or the enemy cutting the road anywhere along the line, there was no plan for bypassing the obstacle. All would come to a complete stop, cutting off the Allied troops to the north.

Prior to the jump General Taylor noted on his map that there was a highway bridge and a railroad bridge over the Wilhelmina Canal in the little town of Best, just west of Zon, the 506th's primary objective. To his thinking the road bridge would make a good alternative in case the main highway was blocked. He pointed this fact out to General Dempsey, the British Second Army commander, who was concerned only with the main thrust by his XXX Corps from Eindhoven to Arnhem and wasn't interested in the small bridges in Best.

After the bridge at Zon was blown up in our faces, cutting the road to Arnhem, General Taylor decided to go ahead on his own initiative and capture the road bridge over the Wilhelmina Canal at Best. This maneuver would give the Allies a way around the roadblock at Zon and secure the division's western flank.

It was believed at the time that the Best bridge was only lightly guarded by a few rear echelon German troops and should present no problem in taking and securing it as an alternate route to Nijmegen and Arnhem. Unknown to our commanders, however, the bulk of the German Fifteenth Army happened to be bivouacked in that area and precautions had been taken by the German command to replace their rear echelon troops with battle-experienced line troops. General Taylor's decision to send only one company on that mission alerted the Germans, who in turn reinforced their troops guarding the bridge in that area.

When the company commander realized they were faced with superior forces, he sent out a call for help and more American troops were sent in. Both sides kept making call after call for reinforcements, escalating the battle to the point where more than a thousand enemy troops supported by tanks were pitted against our 502d PIR supported by British tanks. It was a bitter and bloody battle.

It all started on D day when a platoon from the 502d PIR was ordered to move to Best and secure the bridge. However, the detail was increased to a reinforced company. The 502d's H Company, commanded by Capt. Robert E. Jones, drew the assignment. Plans were quickly made and H Company moved out from Drop Zone B, traveling through the woods in the direction of Best. The company arrived near Best on the Bokstel highway and was immediately fired on by the enemy.

The troopers could see that the Germans on the other side of the canal were receiving reinforcements by truck to make a stand, so they withdrew a short way to set up a defensive position in a wooded area and call for reinforcements of their own. Captain Jones ordered 2d Lt. Edward L. Wierzbowski, the 2d Platoon leader, who had only eighteen men left after the bitter fighting earlier, to reinforce his platoon with men from an engineer platoon and then move out and secure the bridges.

The engineers weren't much better off than Lieutenant Wierzbowski's platoon, having lost nearly half of their men. The combined platoons moved out through a tree plantation full of young pines with open lanes spaced throughout it. A machine gun opened up on them, and the troopers swung wide to avoid it. As darkness settled over the area they began crossing the lanes spaced out between the trees in rushes, a few men at a time.

Private First Class Joe Mann took over as lead scout and led the patrol through the inky blackness. They cleared the plantation and continued on through fields and a small woods and finally to and over a dike to the canal's edge. The platoon headed west along the canal, climbing over and through obstacles until finally Lieutenant Wierzbowski figured they should be at or near the bridge. He moved forward and conferred with Mann. As they talked in hushed tones they suddenly realized they were in the close presence of German sentries guarding the bridge. They silently flattened out and waited quietly for the sentries to move away from them.

After about a half an hour the rest of the platoon began to grow restless, not knowing what had happened or if the lieutenant and Mann were coming back or not. While they sat there wondering what to do next, several German grenades thudded around them in the darkness. Some of the men tried to scramble back over the dike and were hit by machine-gun fire. Others ran back toward the woods. The balance of the men hastily dug in at the base of the dike.

When the shooting and grenade explosions erupted, Lieutenant Wierzbowski and Private Mann made a break and ran back to the platoon. Artillery and mortar shells rained down on them and the platoon withdrew farther back down the dike and dug in again. Wierzbowski got a head count and weapons check. He had three officers, fifteen men, a machine gun with five hundred rounds, a mortar with six rounds, and a bazooka with five rockets.

Captain Jones, who was becoming worried about the reinforced platoon he had sent out to capture the bridge, sent out three patrols and finally a full platoon to look for Wierzbowski and his men. They all were stopped cold by enemy small-arms, artillery, and mortar fire. The rest of H Company remained in the woods where they had dug in. During the night the company sustained thirty-nine casualties.

Back at regimental headquarters, Lt. Col. John M. Michaelis, the 502d's commander, listened to the steadily increasing sounds of small-arms and artillery fire coming from the direction of Best as daylight faded and realized that more than a company was needed to get the job done. With the bridge at Zon blown, taking the Best bridge had become an all-important mission, so Michaelis sent the rest of 3d Battalion to the scene of the action. However, with night coming on it was becoming increasingly dangerous stumbling around in the dark in enemy territory, so 3d Battalion dug in and waited for morning. The Germans also sent in more reinforcements. The battle was escalating.

As the morning sky turned gray, Lieutenant Wierzbowski and his men could begin to make out the shape of the bridge. It was about a hundred feet long and built of concrete. No guards were visible; they had evidently withdrawn just before daylight. A little farther back from the bridge on the opposite side of the canal stood a number of barracks that the Germans had abandoned in favor of defensive positions dug in all around. Every time Wierzbowski sent men toward the bridge, heavy machine-gun and rifle fire would drive them back.

Later in the morning they saw German infantry moving toward them through the trees from the north. They figured they were refugees from the attack 2d Battalion had made earlier. Lieutenant Wierzbowski ordered his men to hold their fire until the Germans were only a few yards away, then they opened up, killing about thirty-five of them. The rest fled back the way they had come.

At midmorning they saw a German and a man in civilian clothes arrive on the far side of the bridge. There was no clear shot at them from their position. The two were there for about half an hour, then left. Suddenly, at about 11 A.M., there was a tremendous explosion and the bridge disappeared. Debris from the bridge rained down on Wierzbowski and his men. Evidently the German and the civilian with him had set a timed fuse on an explosive device (probably an aerial bomb such as was used at Zon) to destroy the bridge.

Joe Mann and a trooper named Hoyle made a feeler patrol and discovered an 88mm ammo dump, which Mann destroyed with rockets from his bazooka. Staying low, the two shot six Germans coming toward them from the north. Mann was hit twice in the arms, so Hoyle took the bazooka and destroyed an 88mm gun set up near the canal about 150 yards away. Mann and Hoyle then made their way back to the rest of the platoon, where the medic treated Mann.

A flight of P-47s passed overhead, circled around, then strafed Wierzbowski's patrol. The men rode out the attack huddled in the bottoms of their holes. Luckily no one in the group was hurt.

Later that same afternoon the Germans again attacked the patrol but were driven back. One of the men out front, Lieutenant Watson, was shot in the groin. Lieutenant Wierzbowski crawled out and dragged him in and the medic treated and bandaged him. The Germans renewed their attack with heavy small-arms, artillery, and mortar fire. Private Onroe H. Luther was hit in the head by a shell fragment and killed. Private Northrop was hit in the base of the spine and rendered helpless. Two more bullets hit Private Mann in the arms. The medic again bandaged Mann's arms but he continued to bleed heavily so the medic put Mann's arms in slings and bound them close to his body in an attempt to stop the flow of blood.

Lieutenant Wierzbowski was going to put Mann back in a safer foxhole with the other wounded but Mann begged to stay with his buddies. Wierzbowski approved his request. Lieutenant Otto J. Laier and Sergeant Betras volunteered to go for help. Betras was wounded and returned a few minutes later. He reported that Lieutenant Laier had been wounded and captured.

Later still, a British recon car and an armored car moved in across the canal. When the Germans opened fire the British gunners blazed away at them with all their machine guns. The Germans quickly ceased fire and left the scene.

Lieutenant Wierzbowski yelled to the British patrol leader to call division and ask for immediate help. The English were unable to get through with their radio, so Wierzbowski began moving his men over the dike to the water's edge, hoping to get to the other side and the safety of the British vehicles with their extra firepower. The English commander yelled for them to stay put. He said he was sure help was on the way. Privates Laino, Waldt, and Koller ventured out on a short patrol and soon returned with three German medics and a wounded German as prisoners. Wierzbowski ordered the German medics to get to work on his wounded, which they did. However, they had no plasma and Northrop was dying from the loss of blood.

An American patrol came across their position but there weren't enough men in it to handle all the wounded. The troopers left after promising to pass along word of the patrol's need and of the destruction of the bridge. Unfortunately, their message became garbled and all that was reported to division was the destruction of the bridge.

The Germans in the meantime had committed more troops to the battle, and the Americans countered with troopers supported by British tanks. Most of the fighting was farther to the west and, as Dame Fortune would have it, none of the reinforcements came anywhere near where Lieutenant Wierzbowski and his men were holed up.

As day faded into night on September 21, a platoon from the 502d PIR's D Company, led by Lt. Nicholas D. Mottola, stumbled into their position and decided to spend the night with them. Mottola and his men dug in on one flank of Wierzbowski's platoon, which in turn adjusted its positions to guard the other flank. During the night a strong German force attacked the position. However, Lieutenant Wierzbowski and his men were so beat and at peace with others on guard that they slept right through it. Meanwhile, Lieutenant Mottola's platoon pulled out and swam across the canal, leaving Wierzbowski's battered patrol to its fate.

The British armored and recon cars heard the shooting and assumed that help had arrived. They left without investigating any further.

Dawn came but was heavy with mist. Lieutenant Wierzbowski looked around, saw that his flank was open where the other platoon had moved out, and observed that the Germans were at that moment mounting an attack and had gotten to within twenty feet of the unguarded side. Several of his men threw grenades but the Germans had already thrown theirs first. When the grenades landed several men retrieved them and threw them all out of the position—except for one that hit the machine gun and exploded in Laino's face. The blast blew one of his eyes out, blinded the other one, and all but destroyed his face. Koller was shot dead. Another grenade coming in struck Laino on the leg and dropped into his hole. Unable to see, he groped for it, found it, and threw it out just before it went off.

Another grenade landed in the main trench next to where Private Mann sat with bandaged arms. His comrades, who were fighting for their lives, didn't notice it. Mann, whose arms were still bound tightly to his chest, yelled "Grenade!" to warn his buddies, then turned and lay with his back on the grenade. It went off and some of the fragments pierced Mann's body and wounded Privates Paxton, Wienz, and Atayade.

Lieutenant Wierzbowski crawled over to Mann's side.

"My back's gone," Mann told the lieutenant, then died.

Out of ammunition and with most of his men wounded, Lieutenant Wierzbowski surrendered his gallant little patrol to the attacking Germans. The survivors were later rescued when elements of the 502d PIR ran into their group, attacked the Germans, and took them prisoner.

Private Joe Mann was posthumously awarded the Medal of Honor for sacrificing himself to save his buddies.

There are several monuments in Holland today honoring Private Mann. Every day for the past fifty-four years the grateful Dutch people and their children and grandchildren have placed fresh flowers at the base of those monuments.

One of the monuments has a photo of him embedded in glass set in the stone. A pelican with its wings outstretched and its beak piercing its own breast stands atop the monument. There is an old Dutch fable that says, "If a pelican goes in search of food and cannot find any for its young, it will return to them, thrust its beak into its own flesh, let it fill with blood, and feed its young."

So it is for the Dutch. Joe Mann gave his blood that they might live in freedom.

5 Northward

September 23, 1944. The road through Zon was jammed with British trucks and drivers. We were ordered to load up. We were heading north and would probably have to fight along the way. We would have to keep a sharp eye out in all directions, keep our ears open, and be ready for combat at all times. The Germans had been attacking in force for the last two or three days from St. Oedenrode to Veghel, Uden, and Erp, capturing the Dommel River bridge in Erp. We moved out slowly, each truck waiting until the truck in front of it had pulled ahead about a hundred yards before following. Maintaining a proper distance between men and/or vehicles in combat is an absolute must at all times. If you bunch up, you become an inviting target for the enemy. In the end, the whole convoy was moving slowly over the main road north out of Zon, heading north to St. Oedenrode, then on toward Arnhem.

There weren't as many civilians on hand in Zon as when we had first arrived. The realities of war had settled in. The Germans were not giving up easily. There would be many battles ahead before Holland would be free of Germans. "Perhaps the Allies will not win," we heard a few civilians remark. "If the Germans return, what will become of us?"

Their concern was not unfounded. The Dutch people had been helping us from the moment we began descending by parachute. They had gone out with horse- and hand-drawn carts to retrieve equipment bundles and men had been scattered around the drop zones. They helped our wounded, set up underground telephone and communication lines, hid and cared for downed airmen, reported on enemy troop positions and movements, and openly displayed their country's flag.

Any one of these offenses against the German invaders was an offense punishable by death. Sometimes the sentence was carried out on entire families or groups of neighboring people. The Dutch people were fiercely patriotic and willingly faced all Nazi threats, giving aid in any way, large or small, to gain their freedom.

We could understand their anxiety, their concern, and their fear. However, if we lost it would mean we were dead or captured. We would give it our best shot. We would not go under without a fight.

Our convoy moved at a fairly rapid pace. Little precaution was taken against the possibility of an enemy air attack. We had no anti-aircraft defense in our convoy other than a .50-caliber machine gun carried in a ring mount on the cab of a few of the six-by-six trucks. The British truckers were confident that our side really did own the air.

Every so often we would see groups of men and women on bicycles moving up and down the roads and through small villages. They were volunteers whose job was to make certain that homes and buildings that had to be evacuated were not looted. Even in total war there had to be some law, some protection for the civilized against anarchy. These people many times faced death when they unexpectedly ran into enemy soldiers. Oftentimes they made their way at their own peril to bring us news of enemy forces they spotted while making their rounds. Their reports on enemy troop strength, disposition, and weaponry proved invaluable.

Our convoy entered St. Oedenrode and moved slowly on through. There were a few civilians in town, all of whom waved at us. We returned their greetings. We swung right onto the main road running to the northeast and continued on for a mile or two. The convoy finally came to a stop a short distance west of a town named Zondveld. We dismounted from our trucks and formed up in battle ranks, then started out on foot toward town. One of the many bicycle patrols reported that a large German force was settling in there and looked as though it was preparing to make a stand. There was nothing strategic about Zondveld that we could see. However, if the Germans wanted it, we had to take it from them.

We began moving cautiously forward with scouts out front, patrols out to either side to protect our flanks, and a rear guard posted. As we neared the houses our scouts spread out and began running from one protected spot to another, always moving forward. We followed at a distance—far enough back to allow us some maneuvering room if we ran into a bunch of Germans who were willing to stand and fight. The scouts entered the village without opposition. We followed them, running from doorway to doorway. We didn't see anyone, not even civilians. There was a feeling of both relief and disappointment; we had geared ourselves up for a scrap during our march here and found nothing. There were no dead Germans to loot, no prisoners from whom we could collect souvenirs. We had nothing to show for our walk across country. Outposts were assigned and we dug in, forming a defensive perimeter around the town. Then we settled in, one man to a hole, ate some cold K rations, and made ourselves as comfortable as possible. It would be a long night.

The Dutch people were usually pretty reliable in their reports. There must have been a large enemy force in the area, but where had it gone? Did the Germans make a show of their presence here to draw us in and then withdraw to prepare for a night attack after we had relaxed in our positions? We didn't know the answers, but we would be ready for anything if and when it did happen.

Nothing did happen. We stayed half awake throughout the night, then formed up at dawn on September 24 and headed back out toward the main road. Our convoy had pulled out the day before, heading north as soon as we detrucked. We cleared the town and continued north on foot. When we reached the main road we turned right and headed in the direction of Veghel.

After a couple of miles we crossed the bridge over the Zuid Willems Canal and entered the city. A halt was called near the center of town and we stood on either side of the road looking around. Veghel seemed to be a fairly large place. Across the street stood a factory with a large painted sign showing gears and the name Veghel. Another sign alongside that one caught my eye. It pictured a bottle of milk. A young Dutch boy of about twelve or thirteen stood at the edge of the road watching us. I asked if he knew where we could get some milk to drink. Although he spoke some English, he did not understand what I wanted. I had seen the factory sign and the large sign with the picture of milk and figured that perhaps this place was a dairy and we could get some milk here.

I asked him again, this time pointing to the signs while pantomiming drinking from a bottle.

The boy nodded his understanding and said, "No, there is no *mellik* here. The Germans take it all."

Not far away, an older man was sitting astraddle a log bench. He was carving wooden shoes. Many of the people wore wooden shoes or a slipper-type wooden shoe with a leather strap over the top of the foot. The Germans must have taken all the leather, too.

Heavy battles had raged here for the last three or four days all the way from St. Oedenrode through Schijndel, Wybosch, and Veghel. The Germans were determined to cut and block the road to Arnhem near its base, clear the Allied forces out in the south, and then deal with the Americans and British isolated in the north at their leisure.

Before it was over the Germans had committed the 107th Panzer and 280th Assault Brigades, both units of the First Parachute Army, and the 59th and 347th Infantry Divisions. Our division committed the 501st, 502d, and 506th PIRs, the 327th Glider Infantry Regiment, and 57mm guns from the 81st Airborne Antiaircraft Battalion.

The enemy succeeded in cutting the main road in three different places and in holding the bridge at Erp over the Dommel River for different periods of time during this engagement. However, by late evening on September 23 the Germans had been driven out of the area except from where they held a roadblock north of Veghel. The 506th PIR's 2d and 3d Battalions, which had attacked south from Uden the day before, held the north end of Veghel and were ordered to attack north to clear the roadblock.

At 3 P.M. the two battalions began their attack north against light opposition and had gone a little over a mile when they met the British Grenadier Guards attacking south on the same mission. With the road to Arnhem again open to traffic rolling north, the 2d and 3d Battalions continued on to Uden, where they took up their old positions.

We resumed our own march northward on the afternoon of the twenty-fourth. We were fired on as we neared the northern outskirts of Veghel, and bullets cracked sharply around and between us. We hit the ground or sought cover in the doorways of the buildings and houses lining the streets. The 1st Battalion charged ahead with men running forward in turn, covering short stretches of ground in quick rushes. Most of the enemy firing came in from our left, from between and behind houses lining the streets, and troopers returned the fire with rifles and machine guns. I ran forward with others of 2d Platoon. We headed north at first, then turned left between some houses on the side of the road where we thought the Germans might be hidden. Hearing several bullets cut close by us, Phillips, Benson, Speer, and I hit the ground at the same time.

Sergeant Vetland was to our far right, and a young Mexican—Salome Alvarado, I think—was up ahead peeking around the rear corner of the house. He took aim at something we couldn't see and waited. He waited motionless there for so long I thought he had fallen asleep. Sergeant Vetland was watching him intently from the corner of another building. Finally, Alvarado fired. He looked back at the rest of us after squeezing the trigger.

"I joost had to keel him," he said apologetically in his thick Mexican accent. "I didn't want to but he kept coming and coming and I joost had to keel him."

Sergeant Vetland, grinning from ear to ear, yelled his congratulations to Alvarado. He told us later that he wasn't sure if Alvarado would kill the man or not. Now he knew he could trust Alvarado with missions requiring someone who could and would shoot to kill. It is surprising how many men, even in the paratroops, don't shoot to kill—or don't shoot at all—in combat. It was all-important to know just who could be counted on when the time came.

Men were again on the move. I ran forward toward another house, cut to the right side, and then raced around the back into a small, open yard. Three Germans were standing there half crouched, grouped closely together, watching the road from around the other corner of the same house. They hadn't seen me.

I took aim and yelled, *"Hacht Hans!"*

The startled Germans turned and looked sharply at me. They immediately dropped their weapons and yelled *"Kamerad!"* in unison as they raised their hands above their heads.

I know my pronunciation wasn't correct, but they weren't about to argue with me over the muzzle of my M1. It would have been easy enough to shoot them all on the spot but I figured someday I might be in the same position, and I hoped an enemy would give me the same choice.

The skirmish did not last long. The Germans who we killed or captured must have been the dregs of the attack force that had been attacking our lines for the last three days. I think they were tired and just about ready to quit anyway.

We turned our prisoners over to the troops in town. None of our men were killed and only one man was wounded in our group. He had been watching an approaching German from the corner of a nearby house. Suddenly a shot from an unseen enemy rang out and the bullet struck the corner of the brick building close to the trooper's head. Brick fragments, not the bullet, tore his eye from its socket. The medics bandaged his head and led him back toward the center of Veghel.

We re-formed and continued our march north, entering the city of Uden later that same day. Again we were assigned defensive positions and again Bielski and I were placed together. We were instructed to set up our lonely outpost near a small house southeast of town—this time without the machine gun. While we were digging our foxhole, the man of the house came out to join us. He spoke fairly good English and soon we were talking like old friends. He told us that German parachutists had landed in this area when Holland was invaded back in 1940.

One of the German parachutists had landed nearby and lay there for several minutes before getting up. The man said the German was quite visibly shaken. When he finally stood up, he felt his legs and arms and, finding no broken bones, drew his pistol and swaggered around, waving the pistol as he ordered all the civilians who had gathered around back into their homes. Bielski and I found the story amusing. It didn't sound at all like one of our drops.

"Why didn't someone shoot the Kraut?" I asked.

"Because," the man replied simply, "no one in Holland is allowed to have a firearm. No one had anything to shoot him with."

The thought of one man with a pistol dominating an entire town seemed incredible.

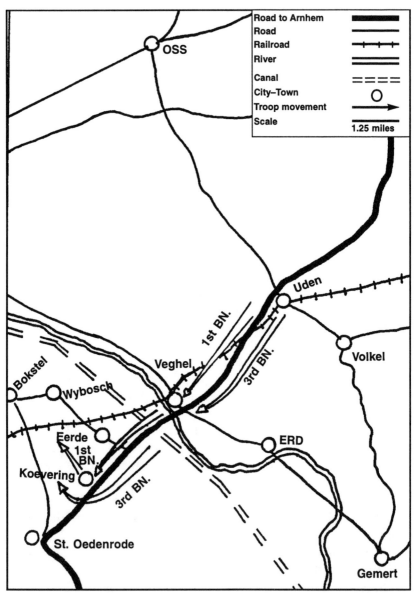

1st and 3rd Battalions Counterattack into Koevering

It was 3:30 A.M. and dark as the inside of a whale when we got the word to get ready to move again. It seems the Germans had launched another attack, this time between Veghel and St. Oedenrode to the south, and had cut the road again. The Germans had cut the road in the area so many times and in so many different places that it kept the entire division busy, with units running from place to place to force the Germans out and reopen the road. The British were supposed to have taken over this job, but they were behind schedule and had not yet done so.

There were radio reports of a lot of English troops ambushed and killed on the road south of Veghel. It was now up to us to get there and reopen the road. The German attacks on our one and only highway north were causing major problems, heavy damage, death, and disruption of vital traffic. American paratroopers, the "fire brigade" having to put out these brushfires, had begun calling it "Hell's Highway."

We moved out heading south, spreading out on either side of the highway ready for instant combat. There was no telling just how far the Germans had expanded their hold on the road ahead of us, what kind of armament they had with them, or when and where we would hit them.

Passing through Veghel we again crossed over the Aa River and the Willems Canal, then continued south toward Koevering. The 3d Battalion covered the left side of the road, while our 1st Battalion covered the right side. As we approached Koevering we could see smoke rising from burning vehicles. It was now late in the day. Soon we saw the destroyed English convoy up ahead. Most of the vehicles were on the eastern side of the road and had been heading north when they were hit.

The 3d Battalion swung farther east and south before heading west, straight toward the Germans. We spread out, getting distance between men. Our platoon crossed over the road to the east and aligned itself with 3d Battalion's right flank. We passed through several fences, tree lines, and fields. Up ahead was a large haystack; we moved toward it. Suddenly rifles and burp guns opened up on us from the haystack. We went to ground and returned fire into and around the haystack. Sergeant Vetland, Charles "Red" Knight, and several others from our 2d Platoon were a little to our right. Again small-arms firing erupted at us. Sergeant Vetland called to Angelo Montrella to drop a mortar shell behind the haystack.

Montrella quickly set up the 60mm mortar and sighted up the tube. Seeing tree limbs overhead, he moved the mortar just enough to clear them, then leveled the sights while telling his assistant to pull the increments and the pin on one shell. It was a short-range shot. He dropped the shell down the tube and the round made the familiar *plong*-like sound and was on its high-trajectory way.

Moments later the shell landed directly atop the haystack and exploded without starting a fire, scattering hay in all directions. We were still receiving fire from the other side. Vetland started laughing, "Not *on* the haystack," he yelled to Montrella. "I said *behind* the haystack."

Montrella laughed, too, and soon we all broke out laughing. Montrella made a slight adjustment and dropped another shell in the tube. The round *plonged* out and moments later landed directly behind what was left of the haystack. At the same moment it exploded we were up and running. Several of us on the left flank rounded the stack on that side and there at our feet lay three dead Germans, killed by the mortar blast. Sergeant Vetland and Red Knight came around from the right, tommy guns at the ready. Several others followed them.

"Let's go!" Vetland yelled. We turned to the east and ran straight toward the road and the wrecked vehicles. The smells of burning rubber, burning oil and grease, and the burnt flesh of the dead were all there. A farmhouse, barn, and outbuildings stood across the street, set back a little way amid some trees. Daylight was beginning to fade; it would be getting dark soon. We wanted to get this over with quick; we didn't relish fighting in the dark of night. I came to the wrecked vehicles and bodies. Others had already crossed the road ahead of me. Flames were still licking up from some of the trucks. Much of the cargo was scattered around, evidence that the Germans had taken time to loot the cargo and the dead after springing their ambush. Bodies were piled atop one another or lay side by side next to the trucks and other vehicles. More than three hundred English soldiers had been killed along this short stretch of Hell's Highway.

Large Cadbury chocolate bars were scattered along the shoulder of the road where they had spilled from one of the ruined trucks. Several partially burned bodies lay on them. I stopped long enough to roll one of the bodies out of the way, then scooped up a couple of large handfuls of the chocolate bars and stuffed them inside my jacket before starting out again. The English had stopped for tea. Five-gallon tins of tea, along with pots and kettles of cooked food, some of which had been spilled or smashed, were in evidence all along the length of the convoy. They never got to finish their meal.

We charged forward, receiving small-arms fire as we crossed the road. German machine guns cut loose with their fast ripping bursts, and rifle fire and strings of 40mm shells came in on us. Speer was behind me, along with Correa, Phillips, and Benson. All of 2d Platoon was here. Red Knight and Sergeant Vetland were up ahead with Cread Marriott, Easly, and Brininstool. Everyone was spread out, running forward toward the farmhouse and barn. The farmhouse was now ablaze in the rear.

Most of our squad headed around the right side of the house before cutting left between the burning house and the barn. The house had evidently been set afire by tracers hitting it. The firelight lit up a large area. For a moment I thought of going around the right side of the barn, but the contrast between the light of the fire and the darkness along that side of the barn caused me to turn to the left, following the others running in that direction. We entered a wooded area away from the farmyard and headed down a lane through the trees.

"There they are! There they are!" Speer yelled, pointing to our left front. I looked but in the growing darkness I could not see anything.

"Shoot! Shoot!" I yelled at Speer. "If you can see 'em, shoot 'em!" Speer had extremely good eyes and often saw the enemy before anyone else did. But he always yelled and pointed instead of firing first. Even in battle he seemed a little hesitant to shoot. We all warned him to shoot first when he hit the ground. That way we'd know the enemy was there. But he would always yell and point.

The enemy opened up on us with a machine gun. They couldn't have been more than a hundred feet away in a dug-in position.

Sergeant Vetland opened up with his tommy gun and Red Knight ran over to join him. We all returned fire. I could see the figures of moving Germans and their muzzle flashes but was unable to make out individual targets, so I just fired into the shadowy group knowing they were the enemy.

Vetland and Knight were standing side by side, singing an old Sunday school song as they blasted away at the enemy: "In my heart there rings a melody, rings a melody, rings a melody. In my heart there rings a melody, rings a melody of love."

Those nitwits, I thought. *How the hell can they be so cool? This is serious business.*

Then someone yelled, "Let's go, let's go, let's hubba hubba one time."

We responded by charging straight at the machine gun as bullets cracked around and between us. I felt bullets pass to the right and left of my head. Later, I discovered three bullet holes in my left trouser leg, just above the boot top. Running straight at the enemy when they opened fire usually unnerved them. They expected men to fall back in the face of point-blank fire and go to ground, but there we were, yelling like madmen and firing as we charged straight into their firing machine guns. They stopped firing, threw up their hands, and began yelling, *"Kamerad, Kamerad, Kamerad."*

We overran their position and found a couple of them lying on their backs on the ground with their hands clasped over their heads. A couple more stood to one side with their hands up, not moving. Several others had started to run but thought better of it and froze in their tracks. Several German bodies lay around the position. We brought the German prisoners back to the burning house and the barn. A few of our men began pushing the Germans around, roughing them up a little while shouting questions at them: "Where are the others? There's more Krauts around here. Where are they? How many more are here?"

The sound of firing increased all around. It was getting darker, and muzzle flashes and tracers were visible in all directions, with ricochets whining off to wherever. More 40mm shells and small-arms fire came in on us. The 40mm rounds came in long, arching, fiery strings, striking among us. Marriott, standing just in front of me, was hit bad and went down hard, moaning as he lay on the ground. Several men called for the medic, who was there almost instantly, tending to Marriott.

Our numbers grew as the rest of A Company gravitated our way, guided by the light of the burning house, all the firing, and our loud voices.

It was totally dark now. Firing from both sides slowed and then came almost to a stop. There was no sense going any farther and getting ambushed. We formed a large defensive perimeter and began digging in for the night. The attack would continue in the morning as soon as it got light. We would clear the area of enemy and reopen the road then.

Sergeant Vetland, with Leon Jackson by his side, came to me and said, "Burgett, come with me." I fell in with them and we walked south along a narrow, two-track road away from the burning house. Vetland said 3d Battalion was to be on our left in the next attack and that we had to make contact with them to consolidate our lines. We walked south through the dark until we came to a road coming in from the east. We could see several 3d Battalion men running hunched over in short bursts from cover to cover, making their way toward us. They must have been held up, for they were just getting here. They hadn't seen us as yet.

We waved and yelled to them that the area was secure and to hurry our way, but they took their time. There was really no telling if there were any enemy hidden in the darkness between us. The three of us waited until several 3d Battalion men began walking in the center of the two-track road toward us. We yelled for them to hurry but they continued to walk at a steady pace.

Finally, Sergeant Vetland told me to wait there and inform them where our lines were, then return. Both he and Jackson left, fading into the dark toward our company's position.

"Hey!" a voice yelled after they were gone.

I looked around but could see no one. I turned back to watch the approaching 3d Battalion troopers, wishing they would hurry so I could get back to my own area and dig a foxhole.

"Hey, you!" a voice shouted. It sounded a little more emphatic this time.

Again I looked behind me, but with all the firing still going on it was hard to tell just where the voice came from.

Finally, the voice yelled in a demanding tone, "Dammit, I'm talking to *you*."

This time I was able to locate the sound. I turned and looked down into the ditch behind me and there, not ten feet away, was a German in a hole with a Schmeisser burp gun pointed right at my back. I knew I was dead.

The man spoke perfect English. "If I surrender to you, do you promise not to shoot me?"

What the hell did he expect me to say? "Yeah, I promise," I replied. "I won't shoot you."

He rose up from the hole without hesitating, laid down the burp gun, and climbed onto the road beside me. I was astonished. He was about six feet four inches tall and very slim. Most Germans were about the same height as us but this man was tall.

The 3d Battalion men were close enough for me to yell at them that A Company was to their north and that we were digging in for the night. After they acknowledged that they understood I turned back to my prisoner. "Come on," I said. "Let's go."

We hadn't gone fifty feet when the German stopped and said, "Would you like some souvenirs?"

"Like what?" I asked.

"Come," he replied.

We went back to his hole. He had two Schmeissers, a sack of grenades, a Luger pistol, and binoculars all laid neatly on the edge of his hole. I looked the stuff over and said, "No, I don't want it."

The German seemed surprised and wanted to know why. He said he thought Americans were the biggest souvenir hunters in the world. Why wouldn't I want these things? I explained that I already had enough to carry. What with extra machine-gun ammo, my personal weapons, and all, I just couldn't carry all the souvenirs I came across. Besides, I figured there would be plenty more before the war was over. We left, walking silently down the narrow dirt road, heading back toward the rest of my company.

Along the way I offered him a cigarette. He accepted one from my outstretched hand and I lit it for him. I smoked one, too, even though it was dark. Lighting up a cigarette wasn't really dangerous at that time because there was a burning house lighting up the area and our men were all over the place. We continued until we reached the A Company area. Men were busy digging in, and I spotted Sergeant Vetland and several others standing in a group, overseeing preparation of our defensive position. He looked up at our approach and exclaimed, "Hey, Burgett, what the hell have you got there?"

I explained what had happened after he and Jackson had left and Vetland told me to put the German in the barn with the other prisoners being held there. I looked over at the barn and saw several other prisoners being herded there. I walked my prisoner over to the large door. A trooper was standing there kicking the Germans as they entered.

"Don't kick this one," I said. "He could have killed me but he didn't. Don't kick him."

The trooper just couldn't help himself. He kicked my prisoner in the butt as he passed, not hard, just enough to let me know that he was going to do what he wanted to do anyway. The tall prisoner turned and smiled at me, and I handed him half a pack of cigarettes. I felt I owed him something. He accepted the cigarettes, waved, and went inside. I remember thinking that he was probably relieved his part in the war was over. I didn't know it at the time, but my part was to last until the very last shot was fired.

I wandered back over to the perimeter and started digging a hole near Bielski and Speer, who were on the machine gun together. It was raining, not hard, but when you stand outside in it all day you eventually get soaked to the skin. We slept and kept watch fitfully that night. Every so often the Germans would fire a long string of 40mm rounds in and around our area. They also lobbed a few mortar shells, although most of those landed outside our perimeter. Their gunner didn't have the proper range.

At long last the sky began to lighten. The firing had died down to almost nothing. Of course that didn't mean the enemy wasn't there, they may just have been waiting for us to show ourselves so they could get a better shot. The house fire had died down to the point where all that was left was smoking ashes. We were hungry. We hadn't had anything to eat in a couple of days because we hadn't been issued any rations while we were on the move.

I remembered the Cadbury chocolate bars stashed inside my shirt and shared them with the others. While we were eating, Speer pointed to the treetops. His keen eyes had spotted a large round ball wedged in the upper limbs. It was a round cheese about the size of a basketball. A couple of well-placed shots into the supporting limbs and the wax-coated cheese fell to the ground and was quickly retrieved. Then we saw several beehives on benches under the apple trees. Bielski and I lifted one of the beehives and killed the bees with burning straw as they came out. We lifted the top off and took out small wooden square frames filled with honeycomb. It was our first meal since leaving Zondveld: honey, cheese, and Cadbury chocolate.

The area to the west of Koevering had to be cleared of enemy. Orders were issued and we formed up in lines of skirmishers and headed into enemy land. We passed through a line of trees bordering a fair-sized field, then moved slowly and carefully across the open area looking for signs of enemy in the far tree line. We saw no one ahead. When we were about halfway across the field a Sherman tank materialized from out of the trees to our left, moved down our ranks behind us, pivoted left, and fell into line, keeping pace with us. Its presence made us feel better. If we ran into a larger force at least we would have a tank to back us up.

Phillips was walking to my left, the tank was to his left, and Benson was to the left of the tank. We had walked about a hundred feet like this when Benson moved around behind the tank to where Phillips was and motioned for me to join them. I moved over to where they were and Benson said, "That's a Kraut tank."

"No way!" Phillips and I exclaimed. "It's a Sherman, it's an English Sherman. Some of them moved into this area yesterday to help out."

"Then how come there's a black swastika painted on the side?" Benson asked.

Phillips and I looked at the tank more closely. Sure enough, there *was* a swastika painted on the side near the bow.

"Hell, I don't know," I replied. We were all still walking toward the tree line ahead, the Sherman keeping pace with us.

Benson moved behind the tank and clambered up the rear onto the deck and then the turret. He began banging on the commander's hatch with the butt of his carbine, yelling, "Come out of there you Kraut bastards! I know you're in there! Come out of there!"

The hatch opened and a German stuck his head out, eye to eye with Benson, who whipped his carbine up and pointed the muzzle right between the German's eyes. The German, looking even more startled than Benson, threw up his hands and shouted at the crew inside. The tank came to a stop and the entire crew came up out of the hatches. Benson forced them down onto the ground and stood with his prisoners, smirking.

"I told you so," he said smugly. "You guys wouldn't listen but I told you so. They are Krauts. Look at 'em."

He was right. They were Germans and that was a captured Sherman tank.

Benson got on his walkie-talkie and told whoever was on the other end that we had some prisoners and a Sherman tank and to come and get them. Phillips and I continued walking with the others. Benson stayed by the tank to guard the prisoners, saying he would catch up with us later, which he did.

Firing suddenly erupted from the tree line to our front. Small-arms fire lanced through our ranks and we hit the dirt as one. Then men were up and running forward, a few at a time, covering each other as they rushed the tree line in short bursts. I saw several Germans to our right front starting to run away from us at an angle. The men in our 2d Squad opened fire on them. All up and down the line the shooting grew to a roar. Incoming fire began to slow, then stopped. I saw another figure moving to my right front and fired at him. He went down, whether from being hit or as a natural reaction to being shot at, I don't know.

We began running and made it through the tree line, where we found another, smaller irregular field on the other side. Most of the shooting from the enemy direction had stopped. We looked in the foxholes that were abundant in this area. Evidently this had been their main line of resistance the day before when the heavier fighting occurred.

Dead Germans were scattered around on the open ground and in the holes. They had been cut down while trying to withdraw. I looked at one German lying crumpled in the bottom of a hole and kicked some dirt in on him. There was a slight movement in response.

"This one's still alive," I said, turning to Phillips and Bielski.

"No," said Phillips, "he can't be alive, he's dead."

"But I saw him move," I argued. To prove my point, I reached down into the hole, got a good grip on the German's coat front, hoisted him up and out of the hole, and dropped him to the ground. The man opened his eyes. We could see that he was in a great deal of pain, but he didn't cry out. Then, without hesitation, as though he was calmly talking to his own comrades, the German explained that he was badly wounded in the leg and couldn't walk. He asked if we could help him.

Someone called for a medic, and one came right over. I saw a watch chain dangling from his front waist and, needing one, I reached down and ripped the watch from him. A quick glance told me it was a cheap one, so I threw it back to him and told him to keep it. I told him he shouldn't have wasted his money on such cheap junk, that it wasn't worth taking. The German gave me a hurt look as he pawed the watch back into his hand and put it in a pocket.

Troopers moved farther out and around. The enemy had pulled out. This was our objective, to clear them from the area and open the road to traffic. We moved about freely; there was no more shooting. We saw the bodies of several paratroopers in some of the holes. All had been shot through the tops of their heads as they had hunkered there low in their holes. They must have been men of the 502 PIR. I wondered what had made them get so low in their foxholes and stay that way, not looking out, allowing an enemy to walk close enough to shoot them straight down through the tops of their heads.

Perhaps it was grazing fire from the 40mm that had fired on us the night before that had caused them to stay low in their holes while the enemy infantry advanced until they were right on top of them. Other than tanks moving through the area over the last couple of days firing their big guns and machine guns, we could think of no reason other than someone walking up on them while they slept.

There was evidence of heavy fighting between tanks and men, both American and German, in this area before we arrived. We spread out in a good defensive line and dug in for the rest of the day and night. It began raining and rained all night. The next day was soggy and quiet, with no enemy action.

We were relieved at 3 P.M. on September 27 and formed up and moved out on foot back to the highway, where we swung north and headed back through Veghel toward Uden, allowing our clothes to dry as best they could while we walked.

We marched through Veghel, then on to Uden in a long, strung out combat formation. We moved through that town to the western outskirts and again dug in. Our battalion set up its CP in town. We were in a quiet sector and remained there on line without any more firefights or serious artillery bombardment until October 2, when again we were ordered to form up and move out.

This time we went to a wooded area outside Groesbeek, just south of Nijmegen with its nine span, eighteen-hundred-foot bridge over the Waal River. It was beginning to get dark as we moved into the woods. We spread out and started to dig in, the machine guns and mortars carefully sited to cover our whole front and the balance of the troopers spread out to give maximum support to our machine guns and mortars. The bazookas were placed in spots where an enemy tank or self-propelled gun might try to break through.

We settled on who would stand first watch and the rest of us relaxed a little. We hadn't done much in the last couple of days except for our walk up here from Uden.

A trooper from another company walked over to us and said, "See that little rise in the ground through those trees over there? Well, that's Germany. I just went over there and took a big crap in Germany."

Suddenly everybody wanted to walk the two hundred yards to the border and relieve himself on German soil. I was no different than the rest. Afterward we boasted that we had crapped all over Germany.

That was just the beginning. In our talks we wondered if we were the first Allied troops to set foot on German soil in World War II. Someone pointed out that the 82d Airborne Division had been in the same area on the first day of the operation, so the first Allied soldier on German soil was probably a trooper from that division. Still, we at least had the satisfaction of going onto German soil to relieve ourselves. Later, some shells landed on our positions. It was a light shelling that produced no casualties. Perhaps the Germans had somehow learned of what we had done and were upset about it.

The glider Sgt. Ed Benecke came into LZ W on D day, Holland, after he and his gun crew unloaded their 75 pack howitzer. The 377th P.F.A. (Parachute Field Artillery) landed in Holland in gliders instead of parachuting in as they did in Normandy in order to have their guns ready for action when they touched down. *(Ed Benecke)*

The fourth German 88 at Zon, mounted directly on the south west corner of the Wilhelmina Canal and the main road at the blown bridge in Zon. There were several silhouettes of Allied planes painted in white on the lower barrel of the gun.

Parachutes of the second drop blossom over LZW on D plus 2, 18 Sept. 1944. This drop was followed by a second lift of gliders. Only 209 of the 385 gliders in that flight arrived on LZ W due to running into heavy fog between England and Holland. *(Epic of the 101st Airborne)*

Dutch civilians wearing their Sunday clothes poured out to greet us as we entered their city of Eindhoven. The closer we got to the center of that city the more the civilians crowded the streets until at times it became impossible to move forward. *(Currahee! regimental scrap book)*

The German 88 could hit high flying B-17's with little effort. It could hit a tank at 3,000 yards and devastate troops in a running attack. The 88 fired flat trajectory high velocity shells that traveled faster than a 30:06 bullet and was by far the most versatile and feared artillery piece of the war. The 88 was usually mounted on a wheeled chassis and was towed along with convoys. *(Epic of the 101st Airborne)*

Advance troops of General Horrocks XXX Corps arrive in Eindhoven, 6:30 P.M. 18 Sept. 1944 greeted by waiting 101st Airborne paratroopers. *(Epic of the 101st Airborne)*

Eindhoven after the Germans had bombed indiscriminately the night of 19/20, Sept 1944, causing more than 1,000 Dutch civilian casualties, more than 200 of which were killed. The British lost a large part of its convoy along with ammo and other needed supplies. *(Currahee! Regimental scrap book)*

Troopers of the 506 Parachute Regiment enter Veghel from the south on their way toward Nijmegen. Fighting broke out as we arrived in the north end of Veghel. After winning that battle we had to retrace our steps to Koevering to beat off German paratroopers. *(Epic of the 101st Airborne)*

British stopped for tea along Hell's Highway somewhere between St. Oedenrode and Veghel and were ambushed by German paratroopers using 40 mm antiaircraft guns, tanks, and small arms. A British soldier stands atop a burned out truck surveying the devastation. *(Epic of the 101st Airborne)*

Older self propelled gun was knocked out near Koevering. This unusual looking gun was not seen much at this later time in the war. The smaller gun was a faster firing weapon with a recoil mechanism atop the barrel. In close quarters it could be devastating. *(Ed Benecke)*

German self propelled gun knocked out of action in one of the many battles near Koevering. This self propelled gun is mounted with a short barreled 75 mm cannon used in close support of attacking ground troops. *(Ed Benecke)*

The area around St. Odenrode, Koevering, and Veghel was infiltrated and attacked many times by the enemy in ambushes and straight forward attacks. This unidentified airborne gunner kills a German tank in a duel on a narrow road. *(Epic of the 101st airborne)*

German half track stripped down and mounted with a smaller field gun. This modified half track mobile gun is mounted with a fabricated armored cab, which wasn't much in the way of protection for the gun crew. Note the American paratrooper directly behind the cab holding a German Schmeisser (Burp gun). *(Ed Benecke)*

General Horrocks XXX Corps halt their miles-long column of Sherman tanks to consult maps on Hells Highway, the only Allied held main road leading to Arnhem, where the British Red Devils 1st Airborne Division were encircled and were systematically decimated by the enemy Panzers. *(Epic of the 101st Airborne)*

The famous Nijmegen Bridge over the Waal River. This bridge was captured intact by the 82d Airborne Division primarily with the bold move of Colonel Reuben Tucker's 504th Parachute Regiment which crossed the 400 yard wide river in flimsy boats in the face of heavy fire to attack and take the far end of the bridge. *(Ed Benecke)*

506 troopers move into positions at the Opheusden rail road station. The troopers are moving from west to east past the station, which means they are probably returning from an attack or patrol action against the enemy. *(Epic of the 101st Airborne)*

"Screaming Meemies" is what we called them. They came in varying sizes and number of barrels. Large diameter mortar shells were electrically fired from batteries of these multi-barreled guns. Volleys of their shells shrieked and screamed in high trajectory from mortar to target, shredding the air and nerves of everyone for miles around. Their impact and explosions were devastating. *(Ed Benecke)*

The most feared tank in the world in its time. The heavily armored Tiger tank was mounted with the dreaded 88 cannon, a combination that was like a miniature land roving battleship. This Tiger met its doom at the hands of paratroopers between the towns of Driel and Elst. *(Ed Benecke)*

This Tiger was killed by British Shermans on the road to Arnhem. Standing dead in the center of the road it was pushed unceremoniously off into the side ditch where it rolled over on its back to do more than just "play" dead. *(Ed Benecke)*

Vengeance is mine sayeth rocket-firing British Typhoons. The scrap piled German tank is mute testimony to the power of the rocket armed Typhoons. Trooper stands next to the wrecked German tank. The crew never knew what hit them.

The rail bridge at Nijmegen was taken by the 82d Airborne at the same time they took the Nijmegen Road Bridge. Both bridges stood for days afterward under constant shelling and bombing by the Germans. The Center span of the bridge was destroyed by a German under water demolition team. *(Ed Benecke)*

One of the many Allied aircraft lost in the battle for freedom. This one went down from German antiaircraft fire near Elst. The author did examine the wreck and found the cremated bones of one crew member still aboard along with the melted lump of nylon of a parachute. *(Ed Benecke)*

Unidentified trooper stands outside his foxhole under a mile marker post which locates his position near the town of Heteren, some thirteen kilometers west of Arnhem, which by this time had long since been overrun by the Germans.

Nearly the full 101st Airborne Division was transported by truck back across the Nijmegen Bridge when relieved from combat in Holland. But a few, like these troopers of the 377th P.F.A. Battalion, were transported by boatload across the Waal River by Canadian Sappers to the Nijmegen side. *(Ed Benecke)*

6 The Island

October 3, 1944. The 506th PIR had spent the night of October 2–3 dug in on a defensive perimeter outside of Groesbeek near the German border. It had rained on and off all night. The wooded area was dark, cool, and wet, not at all comfortable. Our holes were half filled with water, our boots were soggy, our clothes were damp to the skin, and the wood was wet enough that fires were difficult to build and maintain. There was no use complaining, though, all of Holland was just plain wet.

While we were sitting there shivering in our holes, word came down that we would be moving farther north, that there was more fighting in store for us. It became all too clear that the 101st and 82d Airborne Divisions were now being used as regular infantry. As airborne forces we were only supposed to be used to land behind enemy lines and take and hold key points and strategic positions until friendly troops linked up with us. That was supposed to take no more than seventy-two hours, after which we were supposed to be withdrawn to ready ourselves for other important missions requiring swiftness and stealth.

Both U.S. airborne divisions had accomplished all of their assigned missions and more ahead of schedule. We had held the highway open for the approaching British XXX Corps. Unfortunately, the English tankers and infantrymen seemed not to be in too much of a hurry to get to Arnhem, where the British 1st Airborne Division and the Polish 1st Parachute Brigade were no more. They had been allowed to die in place, fighting desperately to hold on for the relief that never arrived.

The road to Arnhem—"The Corridor" as the English called it, or "Hell's Highway" as we referred to it—was now well braced. British ground troops had taken over from Eindhoven, through Zon, Veghel, and Uden, in the 101st's sector, and from Uden, Grave, Nijmegen, and across the Waal River, in the 82d's sector. Our missions had been completed as per schedule and in accordance with the original plan. We were long past due to be relieved from combat in Holland, relieved from service under Monty's command, and returned to our bases to prepare for new vital missions elsewhere in the American sectors that could only be carried out by airborne troops.

Instead, Monty, treating us paratroopers as regular infantry, ordered the 101st north to "The Island," an area bounded on the north by the Neder Rijn and to the south by the Waal River, to bolster his ground troops there. They had run into more Germans than they could handle and needed our help. Shortly after this Monty also ordered the 82d Airborne into the line. He had all but decimated his own 6th Airborne Division in Normandy the same way, ordering them to stay on as regular infantry long after they were supposed to have been pulled out, the way we had been. When September 17, 1944, arrived, the British 6th Airborne Division was still too depleted to join in Operation Market-Garden.

Montgomery had assigned the bulk of his troops the mission of clearing the area around Antwerp, leaving British forces around Arnhem shorthanded. Instead of hammering on through the Arnhem bridge to link up with their comrades on the north bank of the Neder Rijn as the plan called for, they had shifted west to attack the city of Opheusden. Now they were strung out beyond the 82d's protective sector and in dire need of help. Enter the 101st Airborne Division. Our division CP moved to the small town of Slijk Ewijk, just north of the Waal River and a few miles west of the Nijmegen bridge. The troopers wasted no time renaming Slijk Ewijk "Slicky Wicky."

We were ordered to assemble at 1 P.M. The Island was a flat, inhabited area with many orchards and tobacco fields lying between the high dikes built up along the length of the two rivers that flowed around it. It became a bitterly contested piece of Dutch real estate as the Germans and British, and now we Americans, fought to control it.

Another convoy of trucks was brought close to our bivouac area, and we marched out to load aboard with our weapons and personal gear. The roads in the area were narrow, as are most of the roads in Europe, and the drivers would have to turn around in an open field in order to head back the other way. The English drivers were reluctant to do that, though, because the fields were covered with enemy bodies. American paratroopers took over the driving without protest from the English, headed into the body-strewn field, circled wide, and, with trucks following in single file, pulled back onto the road headed in the right direction. Our convoy then moved out, heading toward Nijmegen and the bridge over the Waal River.

The trip was fairly easy. This time there were no throngs of civilians blocking the roads as in the first days of our arrival. The Dutch civilians were still thrilled that we were there, but life went on—and with it the struggle for existence. There just wasn't enough time to celebrate every time we showed up someplace.

We moved into Nijmegen, passing over some railroad tracks. The streets twisted through the city, crossing and recrossing the tracks. Looking to our left we saw a long railroad bridge over the river, then we crossed the tracks again. The low, flat ground that lay between the city and the water's edge looked like a park. There was grass, trees, and no buildings. This green land between the dikes and the river was used as pasture when the river was not out of its banks. The road curved to the right and we passed a café with small round tables set out on the sidewalk. Umbrellas poked up through and over them, shielding the diners from sun or rain. The convoy then swung left, heading out over the massive, eighteen-hundred-foot bridge, which we crossed courtesy of the 82d Airborne Division. As we drove along we could see bullet holes through the steel girders. The holes extended from the surface of the road to twenty feet up. You could not place your hand anyplace on the steel from the road surface to that height without covering at least three bullet holes. What a hell of a fight that must have been for the 82d Airborne's troopers.

A short distance after crossing the bridge we turned and headed west along the north bank of the Waal River, then turned north at an intersection and headed toward the small town of Zetten. On arriving in an area between Zetten and Andelst, the 506th PIR detrucked and the English drivers took over again. Almost to a man the English complimented our men on their driving skill.

After milling around for several minutes we formed up in company and platoon formations near a small house. A line was formed and we entered the front door, received rations from men of the British 214th Brigade, and exited through a side door. I drew a tin of oxtail soup. I will never forget it.

Outside, we joined another short line, where we were issued a ration of tea with milk in our canteen cups. Most of us scattered out, found dry spots to sit, and began eating chow. I opened my can of oxtail soup and found a layer of tallow on top. I probed through it with my trench knife and found oxtail bones.

"That's a hell of a thing," I commented to no one in particular. "Giving a half-starved man a can of tallow and bones." It wasn't as though we could run to the corner store for something else, after all.

I tried to trade off some tallow for a bite of food from one of the troopers who'd drawn a can that contained more food than mine did. No one would trade. After eating the cold tallow I pulled the gristly bone from the can and found a small amount of potatoes with peas and carrots jelled in the tallow. Things were looking better. I finished eating the food in the can, then sucked the gristle from the bone until it was quite smooth. Feeling a little more satisfied, I put the bone in my pocket for later.

There was plenty of compo tea on hand, and most of us went back for seconds. We would have preferred hot coffee, but since we were now drawing rations from the British we would have to make do. From that day on, until we were relieved from duty in Holland, we had our share of bully beef, oxtail soup, and compo tea. The English never went anywhere without their tea. The tea came in five-gallon tins containing tea leaves mixed with powdered milk—thus the name "composition tea," which the English troops shortened to "compo tea." The English brewed this mix by throwing several handfuls of the stuff into five-gallon tins of boiling water, then ladled it out into their individual canteen cups. The tea's strength depended on the size of the hand and how many handfuls were thrown in.

Some troopers with canteen cups partially filled with rum came around to where we were sitting. We asked them where they got it.

"Right there, in front of the house," one of the men replied. "The English always get a daily rum ration after their main meals." We ran to get in line to get our share. The rum was strong—too strong for some troopers, who tried to give their portion to others. Some accepted, most refused. Then we noticed that most of the English added tea to their rum ration. We followed suit. The mixture was much more palatable, although it was advisable not to inhale the steam.

By 6:30 P.M. we had been assigned positions along the perimeter and dug in for the night. The British 214th Brigade, having been officially relieved by us, moved out. The transition was complete by nine and the rest of the night was relatively quiet. A few artillery shells came in but they were nothing to get excited about. We were now officially installed on The Island.

The Island was long, narrow, low, and flat. Most of it was below river level, and the German-held side of the Neder Rijn was hilly and much higher. They could therefore look down on us from their higher vantage points and zero their guns in, allowing them to bring heavy artillery fire down on us no matter where we went or what precautions we took. We were never out of their sight or range, so we were compelled to move at night. The enemy also had heavy armored and infantry units dug in along most of the length of the Neder Rijn dike opposite from us. This was not the best military position to be in. Why the hell had the English taken this part of Holland when their original mission was to get to Arnhem? Now that it had become a killing field, Monty pulled his own troops out and ordered us to occupy The Island.

The morning of October 4 came without incident. The 2d and 3d Battalions of our regiment were ordered to march to Opheusden to relieve the British there and left that same morning. On reaching Opheusden, the 2d and 3d Battalions took over the British positions along the main line of resistance (MLR). Before leaving, the British assured our brother paratroopers that this was a quiet sector. The only activity was an occasional small German patrol snooping around.

"If you don't bother them, everything will be just fine," they said. The British then pulled out, taking most of their tanks with them but leaving plenty of artillery in support. That meant our regiment was manning the front in the vicinity of Opheusden without the benefit of a full complement of armor to back us up.

Our 1st Battalion stayed in regimental reserve on the fourth. We received our three English meals in tins, drank compo tea, and forced ourselves to enjoy our rum ration.

The Germans, as though knowing the British had pulled out with their tanks, hit us with a sudden, ferocious, all-out attack along the entire line in Opheusden at 6 A.M. on October 5. Volleys of artillery and mortar shells thundered all along our front. They were joined by "Screaming Meemies," electrically fired six-barreled mortars that got their nickname because of the loud, hollow, screaming sound they made. They came out of the barrel and cut a high trajectory through the air before coming down on their target, shrieking like giant wildcats in a fight.

The loud explosions around us were punctuated by great flashes of orange fire and pillars of black smoke rising skyward. The ground shuddered and shook from the impact of the barrage. The bombardment went on throughout the attack, walking forward as the German troops advanced.

The attack continued in full force with infantry backed by armor. What we at first thought was a reinforced German infantry company actually turned out to be the entire 363d Volksgrenadier Division, reinforced by a regiment of field artillery, tanks, and a battalion of engineers. The main thrust was in 3d Battalion's sector. A full company of Waffen SS troops crossed the river and attacked into 2d Battalion's lines but was driven back. The fighting was hard and brutal. At least two troopers were completely dismembered, their bodies blown apart by artillery fire. Many more were killed or wounded. The aid station set up in the old windmill became overburdened within an hour.

Colonel Sink, our regimental commander, visited 3d Battalion at 8 A.M. and asked the men to hold on until our battalion arrived to relieve them. By 8:45 the 3d Battalion had been forced to commit its reserve to the battle. The 363d Volksgrenadiers pounded into 3d Battalion's lines but the troopers held against the on-slaughts. The Germans redoubled their efforts, swinging flanking troops and tanks to the north and south, forcing 3d Battalion back to the eastern edge of Opheusden, a distance of about four hundred yards.

Our 1st Platoon had been dispatched on the double to 3d Battalion's sector to give support. The 2d Battalion was fully engaged and could not spare any men to help 3d Battalion, so word came down for us and 3d Platoon to pack up and march to Opheusden as fast as possible.

On arriving at the city's outskirts, 3d Platoon continued into town and into 3d Battalion lines. Meanwhile, we were told to dig in near the Dodewaard-Opheusden railroad station, where we remained in reserve.

Before long 1st Platoon became separated from the rest of 3d Battalion. Sergeant Henry Boyd, the acting platoon leader, was wounded and Sgt. Sam Sutherland took over command of the platoon. Around 2:40 P.M. we were called up out of reserve to attack through G and H Companies to retake the ground that had been lost to the Germans.

We quickly saddled up and moved out in combat formation along the narrow roads, angling northward to the center of Opheusden to avoid a running shoot-out with the Germans on our way to relieve 3d Battalion. We made our way through heavy shelling and narrow, winding streets, arriving at 3d Battalion's location around three to begin our attack.

Our regiment was spread out along a 4,500-yard line extending from south to north all the way from the Waal River in the south to the Neder Rijn dike in the north.

We hit the ditches running. Artillery shells screamed in and mortar shells rained down. Screaming Meemies joined in, shredding a man's nerves with their shrill sound of death. Still we made our way forward. Some of our men were wounded and some were killed but there was no time to stop to help. Sergeant Vetland, Red Knight, Lieutenant Muir, and most of the other leaders were up ahead, as usual. Sergeant Brininstool, our squad leader, was with us. Phillips,

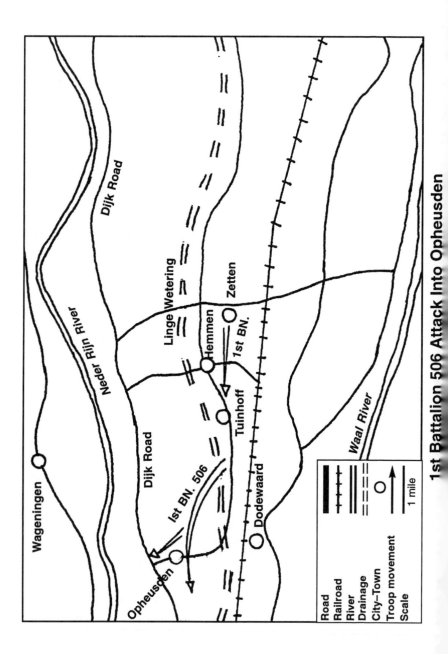

1st Battalion 506 Attack Into Opheusden

Bielski, Correa, Speer, Woolf, and I were moving forward with all the rest, bent over low, hitting the ditches, running in short bursts from here to there—wherever there was even the slightest cover. At the end of one street, men were turning left and funneling through and between two houses. We followed them. All the while artillery continued to fall around us. Still we went forward. I exited from between the houses and found myself with several others behind a short, low brick wall that ran from the corner of one of the houses to a main street. A German machine gun was shooting in fast, ripping bursts amid the sounds of rifle fire. Bullets splattered the walls and pavement around us. Two troopers crouched behind the wall both poked their heads up at the same time, and the machine gun blasted out a fast, ripping burst. They both ducked back down at the same time.

"Don't do that!" I warned them. "That Kraut is going to blow your heads off."

"Naw," one of them replied. "He can't hit a damned thing. We've been trying to see where he's shooting from. As soon as we get a fix on him, we'll kill him."

The man in front of me ducked low and ran out across the street through heavy firing to the corner of another house, where he took cover, then peeked around the corner to see if he could spot the enemy gunner. Another trooper darted across the road, again drawing fire from the enemy gunner. Just then the two troopers behind the short wall again stuck their heads up side by side.

"That gunner is going to figure out where he's hitting and he's going to blow your heads off," I again cautioned.

"Naw, he can't hit anything," one of them said, and laughed.

The German gunner chose that moment to squeeze off another burst and the bullets found their target. The two troopers' helmets flew into the air and brains spattered the ground behind them. Both fell dead, the tops of their heads blown away.

"We'll get that son of a bitch," another man said. "Bring a bazooka up here."

The call went back from man to man: "Bazooka up front! Bazooka up front!"

A big man who turned out to be Charley Syer worked himself forward between the houses with his bazooka.

"Can you hit that house at the end of the street?" a man asked.

"Yeah, I could, but I don't have any rockets," Charley replied. "Anyone got a rocket?"

No one had a rocket. Each trooper usually carried a couple of rockets, a couple of mortar rounds, and a box or two of machine-gun ammo, but right now not one man had a bazooka rocket. The call went back down the line: "Does anyone back there have a rocket? Just one damned bazooka rocket?" Not one was to be had. Charley had used all of his rockets against enemy armor.

Another machine-gun burst hit the brick wall and the front of the house and I ran headlong toward the other side of the street while the gun was trained on the wall. The two troopers who had crossed over ahead of me were well hidden behind the house. I headed straight at the open front door and dove headfirst through it. Evidently the house had been used as a neighborhood store, for there was a counter across what had once been a living room. The machine gun fired a long string of rounds through a large window opening without glass in the front of the store and I leaped over the counter, landing on my back. Dust, plaster, wood, and bullets sprayed in all directions inside the room. Two more times the machine gun blasted the storefront. I continued to lie on my back behind the counter, watching the room being shattered. Finally the firing shifted back to the street. Glancing around me, I noticed on a shelf in the counter a small wooden plaque with a carved wooden shoe and the name "Nijmegen" painted on it, and a spoon made from a Dutch coin. Acting on impulse I grabbed them and stuffed them into my large side pocket. I don't know why; it was just an impulse.

Another trooper dove into the room and I yelled, "Behind the counter, quick!"

The man came over it headfirst, landing beside me just as another machine-gun burst chopped through the room.

At his suggestion we searched the house together, looking for a way around to get at the machine gunner. We went to the basement and found a window in one wall facing toward the enemy. We opened it and across a narrow space between houses saw another basement window. We removed our musette bags to carry by hand in order to make it through the small window. I boosted him up and he went out of the window, then turned and helped pull me up and through. We busted the glass out of the basement window in the house next door and crawled inside. We crossed the basement and exited the other side the same as we had in the first basement, only with me leading this time. We went through an upstairs window in the next house and made our way through the rooms, exiting through a window on the other side. Again I led the way. We crawled into the basement of the next building and went out the other side with him first and me following close behind. We found ourselves in a small, brick-paved courtyard. The bricks had been laid in an intricate swirling pattern. The sun was shining brightly. We had to cross the opening fast.

The other trooper was about twenty feet ahead of me, running hard toward a brick wall at the opposite side of the courtyard when a single shot rang out, loud and sort of muffled in the wall-surrounded courtyard. The trooper, I don't even know his name, pitched forward hard, blood spreading out in a halo around his head on the red bricks. I had been in many attacks before and I knew better than to stop, but for some reason unknown to me I couldn't resist stopping to stare down at his body. A voice screamed inside my head, "Move! Don't just stand here. Move, or you'll be dead too."

I took off running toward the wall, expecting at every step to feel the impact of a bullet slamming into my head or body. There was no shot that I knew of, and I made it safely to the wall, where I crouched low, breathing hard.

Speer suddenly appeared beside me, sliding hard on his knees. "You okay?" he asked.

"Yeah," I replied. "I'm okay. We've got to get to that Kraut with the machine gun." I looked down and saw I was still carrying my musette bag. Speer helped me fasten it back to my harness.

Then, without hesitation, Speer took off running to the next spot. I followed. We continued in that manner, leap-frogging from house to house until we met up with Lieutenant Muir, Sergeant Brininstool, Phillips, Bielski, Ski, Correa, and several others who had made their way around from another direction to this same point, hoping to snag the German machine gunner in a pincers move.

We knew he was close. I looked across the street and saw what I thought was the German gunner's vantage point. Then he fired and we saw the dust rise from the pavement, kicked up by his muzzle blast. He wasn't where I'd thought he was. He was inside a building firing through a small opening hacked through a thick masonry wall facing down the main street. I fired a couple of rounds at the opening hoping to ricochet a bullet into him but the angle was too great and I could not bounce a bullet in it. Others tried, too. It was impossible. Still the gunner fired.

Finally he stopped. Maybe it was to reload or to survey his handiwork or to assess the situation. I don't know. All I know is he stopped firing for a moment.

"Hey you," I yelled. "Give up. Surrender."

"Why the hell should I?" the gunner replied in perfect English.

"If you don't, we'll bring some tanks up here and blast you out."

"You ain't got no damned tanks and we know it. The Englanders took them all back with them. You ain't got no tanks."

"Where did you learn to speak English so well?" I shouted, stalling for time to allow my comrades to make it around to his hiding place.

"I got more time in New York City than you have, you jerk," he replied. "Now come and get me."

It was true. The British had taken nearly all their tanks with them when they left. When we asked for tank support coming into Opheusden, they could spare only a few. They were probably overburdened by the need for tanks elsewhere. The German was right. We had no tanks, and he knew it. But the British artillerymen stayed with us, and they were masters at using their guns.

Our squad made its way around through narrow passageways between the buildings with Phillips and me leading. Finally we came to the rear of the building the machine gunner was firing from. Speer, Bielski, Correa, and the others covered the streets while Phillips and I rushed the back door, which was open. We ran straight through the house to the front. No one was there. We found the hole that had been hacked in the masonry wall through which the German had been firing. He'd had a perfect view of the main street we had to come up or cross. A large pile of spent cartridges lay on the floor at the opening. The German and his machine gun were gone.

He'd known we were coming for him and waited until the last moment to slip away, timing his escape perfectly.

Phillips and I both cursed. We both wanted that smart-mouthed son of a bitch. I kicked a table and swore. Phillips just stood there cursing. We searched the building from the attic to the basement. It was empty. The German had beaten us. The worst part of it was, the German knew it.

Lieutenant Muir formed us up again and we spread out to the east and west of the road to make a sweep as we headed north to join the rest of A Company. Sergeant Brininstool told Phillips and me to take the right side of a brick wall. Others would take the left side. We moved out. It was lonely with just the two of us following along beside the wall through backyards and narrow passageways. At one point we encountered several brick huts attached to the wall that we had to climb over. While we were on the roofs of these structures we searched the other side with our eyes but saw nothing of friend or enemy. We climbed down and continued making our way forward. I thought we were going too far, which we were. We were heading alone deep into enemy territory but Phillips wanted to search farther, so we went on. At one point Phillips climbed over the wall to reconnoiter while I covered him. He was gone so long that I became worried and went over in search of him. We met as he was returning. Both of us retraced our steps along the wall back to where the rest of the platoon waited.

Word came down that our battalion was taking over 3d Battalion's positions. As soon as we arrived, 3d Battalion would move out, heading south. Our battalion would occupy the line extending from the south at the Dodewaard Station, through Opheusden, north to the Neder Rijn dike. The 2d Battalion's line would tie in with us on our north flank at the dike and extend east along the dike to where it contacted the western end of the 501st PIR's lines. The 3d Battalion's new line would extend from the southern end of our line at the Dodewaard Station south to the Waal River.

A Company was assigned the northernmost part of the 1st Battalion line. Our 2d Platoon would set up on the south side of the dike itself, making us the northernmost unit on the MLR. Heavy shelling continued as we moved out with Lieutenant Muir leading, filtering our way through Opheusden. We came to a sort of courtyard where three houses fronted the street, the middle house set back from the street forming this small court between the other two houses. Men were moving into the small yard and then walking single file through a narrow passageway between the two houses on the right to pass through to the other side. Without thinking we began to bunch up in the small courtyard.

Too late we heard the screaming of shells coming in. There was no place to go, no ditch, no holes in the ground, we couldn't even enter the buildings before the shells were on us. The shells struck high on three brick walls, the explosions showering us with dust and bits of rubble. Fire and smoke filled the courtyard and our lungs. Sparks showered over us from shrapnel ricocheting from wall to wall. We were in shock from the heavy concussion. Men staggered drunkenly and milled about, then righted themselves. For reasons unknown to us not one man was hit, not even a scratch. After that we funneled through the narrow opening faster than a stick leaving a plane on a jump.

From there we made our way to the dike running through the northeast part of the city, where we were to set up a defensive line along our side of the dike as far as our platoon could safely stretch. Our squad drew a large three-story house set amid several others that overlooked the dike into enemy territory. However, the enemy, being on higher ground, had a better view of us than we did of them.

I went first, feeling my way down the street. It had become dark in a strange, jumbled city that we shared unequally with the enemy, they having the lion's share. I moved forward guided by the silhouette of the roof against the lighter skyline. Phillips followed me, keeping a close eye to our rear as well as to both sides. I finally located the rear entrance. It was built in sort of an alcove of an overhanging roof with adjoining houses abutting the back corner.

Just as I reached for the door a German fired several long bursts from a Schmeisser burp gun at me. Bullets cut through the air all around my head and body, striking the wall and the door in front of me. I pushed the door open and dove inside. A dog barked and growled viciously in the dark, snapping and snarling. I leaped back outside and the German fired several more long bursts. Again I dove back inside. Phillips came crashing into the dark room with me, chased by long, ripping bursts from a machine pistol.

"What the hell's going on?" he asked breathlessly.

Again the dog snarled in the dark room. Phillips said he would rather take his chances with the German with the burp gun. We both edged back out of the door. The German fired again. He was somewhere in the rooftops of the adjoining buildings. We both emptied our M1s at every spot on the roofs where a sniper might be able to hide. We reloaded and fired, then reloaded again. This time we waited. There were no return shots. We circled in and around the other houses. No more shots and no signs of an enemy. I became angry.

"Where in the hell is that damned mongrel dog?" I mumbled under my breath. "I'm going to blow his damned head off." I went back inside with my rifle at the ready, safety off.

I could hear the dog at the far end of the room. He had settled down some and was growling quietly. Finally my eyes became accustomed enough to the dark that I could see the vague shape of the dog in a chair. As I moved slowly toward him he put his head down and became quiet. I reached forward and held the back of my hand for him to smell. He was shaking so bad he could hardly put his head forward. The poor little bastard was scared to death. He wasn't that large, in fact he was pretty small. I picked him up and he shook so hard he almost went into convulsions. Phillips came in and began talking to the dog. It calmed down, joyous at having found a friend.

The rest of our squad came in behind Luke Easly. They all made a fuss over the dog, feeding him scraps of K rations and petting him. The little cur had almost gotten me killed by that damned German out there on the roof with a burp gun. Lieutenant Muir came in and we set about searching the house. Finding it empty, we set our machine gun up on a large wooden desk in front of a window in a second-floor room overlooking the dike. We made up a guard duty list for the machine gun and for two men to stand watch outside while the rest of us took different rooms in the house to get some sleep.

The rest of the night passed without incident. We had no more trouble from the sniper with the burp gun. I wondered what had happened to him. Perhaps we had killed him and his body was lying somewhere on the roof. We didn't bother to climb up there to look. It really didn't matter; he was just another German.

Dark clouds scudded overhead as dawn broke on October 6. We explored our surroundings in the daylight. A large, elongated earthen mound of sorts was to the left of our house as we faced the dike. We investigated and discovered it was a homemade bomb shelter. Judging by its size, we figured it had probably been built by several families to serve as a refuge during air raids and for such cases as now. However, most of the civilians had moved out to neighboring towns when the Germans and English first clashed here several days before.

There was only one entrance to the bunker, in the end facing our outpost. Inside, a long bench stretched from end to end on either side. It was a perfect shelter, better than any foxhole we could have dug. Our whole squad, except for the two men manning the machine gun upstairs, stood looking it over. While we were standing there we heard the sound of incoming shells. They were headed right for us. As we ran for the bomb shelter I called for the dog, but he just stood there.

Inside, we heard the first shells hit, exploding in shrapnel-spraying violence. The dog went crazy, leaping about, whirling around and screaming, then between volleys he gained some control and came fast when I called, running through the open door and leaping into my lap, where he cowered, shivering. We closed the door and waited until the artillery stopped.

After the barrage we went back outside, careful not to stray too far from the bomb shelter. Again we were hit with a heavy volley of shells. Several times that day we were hit with artillery. We soon noticed that the dog would perk up his ears and run to the shelter just before we heard the incoming rounds. After that, whenever we saw the dog's ears go up and he would start to run for the shelter, we would drop whatever we were doing and run, too. This gave us a two- or three-second edge over what we'd had before—seconds that may have saved someone's life.

Later in the day we were standing around talking when we saw the dog's ears perk up and he started running. We all ran with him, en-

tering the shelter as a mob. Several troopers were ahead of me and
Lieutenant Muir was across from me. Ski had a folding-stock carbine
across his midsection with a finger on the trigger, and when he sat
down it went off. The report sounded like a cannon in the confines
of the bunker. A trooper about three men away from me let out a
yell. The bullet had struck him square in the chest and he was bleeding. Lieutenant Muir moved over to him and tore his shirt open. A
neat bullet hole was centered in his chest. We made room on the
bench and laid him down on it.

"Am I dying?" the trooper asked.

"No," Lieutenant Muir assured him, "you'll be okay." Then he
turned to me and said, "Burgett, get to the windmill and bring back
some plasma, fast."

I took off out the door. Shells were raining down, the explosions
erupting in volleys, shrapnel flying in all directions. There was no
time to waste. I took off running back into town and headed for the
windmill. As I crossed one street a volley of shells blanketed the area,
tearing houses, walls, and everything to rubble. I hit the ground
alongside a brick wall as shrapnel whined overhead, showering me
with sparks when the hot metal fragments struck brick and stone.

Again I ran. It was one of the heaviest barrages we had sustained
since our arrival in Opheusden, and I wondered if it might be the
prelude to an enemy attack. I kept running until I reached the windmill aid station. The medics were swamped with wounded from the
shelling. They did their best, grading the casualties as soon as they
were brought inside.

"This one'll make it. . . . Maybe this guy'll be okay. . . . Nope, this
one ain't gonna make it."

The ones they judged would survive were given priority, and they
worked quickly to get them patched up and out of the way so as to
make room for more casualties. The ones that weren't going to make
it waited. After a while, usually not more than a few minutes, they
were taken outside and placed on the dead pile.

I finally got someone's attention and had to argue to get a bottle
of plasma. It was scarce, precious, not to be given away without good
cause. I finally got a bottle and took off running again. The shells
were still coming in. I figured there must be something big in the
works. I raced through the rubbled streets and finally made it back

to the bunker. I quickly ducked inside and handed the plasma to Lieutenant Muir.

"You're too late," he said and stuck the plasma bottle in his musette bag.

Orders came down that we were to assemble with the company. An attack was planned. The British were sending troops up to help us clear the Germans from the west side of Opheusden. I went upstairs to help with the machine gun and ammunition. I found Bielski trying to remove the belt but it was jammed and wouldn't come free. We each tried several different ways to get it loose without success.

Luke Easly entered the room and, after asking what was taking so long, said, "Here, let me show you how to unstick the damned thing. We've got to get going."

We suddenly knew what he was going to do and yelled, "No!"

It was too late. Luke pulled the trigger and sent a long string of bullets and tracers into enemy territory. I grabbed the gun and ran with the long belt of ammo trailing behind me. We headed for the stairs, bolting down several steps at a time. An 88mm shell screamed in, skimmed the top of the dike, tore through the front of the house, hit the stairway below us, and exploded. The whole inside of the house was torn apart. All I saw was splintered wood, plaster, and dust as we tumbled downward through the chaos caused by the blast.

We came to a stop between the basement and the first floor, mixed in with a pile of debris that used to be a wooden stairway and the walls of the house. Little by little each of us extracted ourselves and helped the others out of the mess. We made it outside and into the bomb shelter. No more shells followed. Miraculously—aside from minor cuts, scrapes, and bruises—no one was hurt.

We moved out with our dog, "Shrapnel," following. We named him Shrapnel because of the way his ears would perk up and he would start running whenever he heard incoming—a sure sign that there would be plenty of shrapnel flying around very shortly. From there we made our way back into Opheusden and took up our assigned position in the attack line.

7
Withdrawal

October 6, 1944. A British brigade of three hundred men was to attack west through the open land on our battalion's left (southern) flank, leaving us with the house-to-house street fighting through the center of Opheusden. I certainly didn't envy the British. Attacking across open ground in full view of an enemy occupying higher ground with superior artillery definitely was not the best military position to be in for survival. We spread out approaching the approximate center of the city.

The British 5th Battalion, Duke of Cornwall's Light Infantry (DCLI), formed up in lines of skirmishers to walk shoulder to shoulder across the open fields. It seemed a very foolish command to us. A barrage from the English artillery fell on the enemy's positions for a full fifteen minutes. The order to start the attack was passed down our ranks at 1:45 P.M. The artillery lifted and we moved out, heading into enemy territory.

Enemy artillery came screaming and moaning in from the west of Opheusden and from the north side of the Neder Rijn. Screaming Meemies added their high-pitched, howling shrieks to the din and 81mm mortars began exploding in our ranks and those of the British. Many of the British went down but still they pressed forward, closing the gaps blown in their lines by the barrage. They marched steadily on, firing their Enfields from the hip, working the bolts, and firing again. The English soldiers were brave to a fault, staying in line and moving forward through the crush of artillery, machine-gun, and small-arms fire. They marched unwaveringly to their deaths. This sort of attack went out with the bloody assaults of our Civil War in the 1800s. Their major had ordered a very foolish maneuver, showing total disregard for his men's lives. But he wasn't in the lines of skirmishers.

Meanwhile, we ran forward in short rushes, diving into ditches, holes, and doorways—anyplace that offered cover as we made our way forward. We were suffering casualties, too, but not like the English.

The western half of Opheusden was filled with Germans but we did not meet them in force in this attack. They were pulling back in front of us, allowing us to move forward and filling the vacuum with artillery barrages that took a steady toll on us as we went deeper into their territory. John "Whiskey" Wisniewski, Jackson's best buddy, was hit hard and went down. The call "Medic, up front!" sounded. Whiskey died in the windmill several hours later. Several others were hit and wounded, and still others were killed outright. Our company commander, 1st Lt. Bill Kennedy, was wounded and evacuated. First Lieutenant Patrick Sweeny took over for him and we continued on. This battle had become a war of artillery. Men on both sides were being chopped to pieces by artillery, seldom closing with each other in one-on-one combat.

The Germans began sending troops to the right and left around our flanks in an effort to envelop us. We pulled our flanks in and folded them back to protect us there. The British on our left were no more. They had been decimated, leaving us exposed on that flank. Our attack slowed. More mortar rounds rained down on us since they were no longer needed to hit the British lines. Finally our attack came to a stop. The intense artillery pounding we were taking was too much to withstand. We were forced to withdraw.

Orders came down for A Company to move to the right and take up defensive positions to hold the enemy back while preparations were made to evacuate the wounded in the windmill. What riflemen could be spared from the lines were pressed into caring for and moving the wounded, who would be leaving along the northern dike road when the time came. A Company moved out to meet the enemy.

We came out of the city into a field growing high with tobacco. The shelling increased and shrapnel cut along close to the ground and sliced high in the air. More men were wounded and killed. We hit the ground, Phillips just ahead of me. I saw deep-rutted tire tracks left by the dual wheels of a German truck that had passed through here while the ground was muddy. I crawled forward, squeegling down into the length of the track, lowering my body height about three inches. That three inches may have made the difference between a piece of shrapnel severing my spinal column or not. I called to Phillips to do the same. He did.

Most of the time I really never thought much about the shrapnel whizzing past. Just hearing it had never really bothered me, but now I could see it cutting tobacco stalks in long rows like a scythe, just inches in front of my face and alongside me. I had never before fully realized just how much shrapnel flew outward from an exploding shell. Now, with multitudes of shells hitting all around, cutting down entire rows of tobacco plants at a time in full view, I was dumbfounded—and scared.

The artillery finally let up and we crawled a hundred yards or so forward to dig in. We could see a road just in front of us. A few houses stood several hundred yards to our left. While we were digging in we began receiving rifle fire from a small house in the field to our left. We returned fire but the house had sturdy walls and our rifle fire did little harm. I always carried a clip of tracers in the front left pocket of my ammo belt and a clip of incendiaries in the pocket next to it. I told Phillips to get ready and keep watch, then I loaded the clip of incendiary rounds into my rifle. Taking aim at the roof I fired three rounds. A short time later smoke began to curl up from the roof. I fired two more incendiaries and within a few more minutes the fire began to spread. I reloaded with armor-piercing ammo and waited. Soon the whole roof was ablaze and flames began spreading down into the house. A little while later a German ran from the left rear of the house and angled across the open field. Phillips and I fired several quick rounds together and the German went down hard, not moving. The house was engulfed in flames at this point. We finished digging in.

Bielski came over and asked if he could dig in with me.

"Yeah," I said. "Get your shovel out and make the hole bigger." He did and we settled in to await orders, the Germans, or whatever else might come our way.

During the night Sergeant Vetland told Red Knight to go west down the road and see if he could find just how far away the enemy was dug in and maybe how many there were of them. Knight took off alone into the darkness. He preferred it that way. Unknown to us, Knight returned much later with several prisoners. A little after that Bielski nudged me and said he heard someone talking and he thought they were Germans.

"Are you sure?" I asked.

Bielski rose up from the hole and listened, then dropped back down and whispered, "Yeah, I could hear several Germans talking."

We whispered to each other about what to do. How to alert our comrades in other holes? We wondered how the enemy had penetrated our lines to this point without others knowing. We decided to crawl forward slowly, get a bead on the Germans, and call for them to surrender. That would also alert our comrades.

While we were deciding on our course of action there was a loud explosion followed by screams, yells, curses, and bursts of tommy gun fire. There was more screaming, and then we clearly heard German voices screaming, *"Nein! Nein! Nein!"*

Bielski and I were up and running toward the sounds, as were others. Red Knight was writhing on the ground with his tommy gun still in one hand. He had several wounds in his body. Sergeant Vetland was standing nearby, but barely. He was staggering around with his tommy gun in hand. Several dead and dying Germans lay on the ground in a group. One of them gasped, *"Nein,* it wasn't us." Then he died.

As we helped Vetland he explained that Knight had brought the Germans in as prisoners and they were interrogating them when one of them evidently threw a grenade. Red said that when the grenade went off and he was going down he started firing, hoping to get as many as he could before he went under. Ted Vetland did the same but remained standing even though he sustained multiple wounds to his face, arms, body, legs, and feet. Medics were called and Red Knight and Ted Vetland were carried back to the windmill first-aid station.

We all returned to our holes, everyone keeping on alert.

We were still awake at the first hint of daylight on October 7. I couldn't recall having eaten anything since we'd been in the house on the dike. Rations didn't come around very often, and I would have welcomed a can of oxtail soup at that point. Then I remembered the bone I had put in my pocket back in Zetten. At least it would be something to chew on. Only I couldn't find it. It was lost. Or perhaps I had given it to Shrapnel and just didn't remember doing so.

Phillips had crept to the edge of our hole and was kneeling there to talk with Bielski and me. I was looking beyond Phillips when a movement on the road caught my eye. Something big was moving very slowly up the road.

"Look at all those bushes moving," I said. It still hadn't dawned on me what I was looking at.

Phillips looked nonchalantly to his left, studied the road for a moment, and said, "Bushes hell, those are tanks!" With that he went scurrying on his hands and knees for his own hole.

The tanks were well camouflaged with leafy bushes and tree limbs. The first one was a huge Tiger, followed by several Panthers. They were moving at a walking pace. When they were exactly parallel with us they stopped. They knew we were there but the tobacco plants hid us from their view. The turrets swiveled until the big guns were pointing in our direction, then we saw the troops. There was at least a battalion of German infantry behind the tanks, looking for us.

"Get the CP on your walkie-talkie and ask permission for us to withdraw from here," Sergeant Brininstool shouted at Benson.

Benson tried but was unable to raise the company headquarters or anyone else back in town. His walkie-talkie wasn't working again. What else was new? Most of the time Benson carried the damned thing around in a rubberized bag, all broken down while he was working on it.

"Benson," Brininstool said, "go back to town and ask permission for us to pull back from this position."

Benson took off, snaking low through the high tobacco plants. We waited, watching the Germans, who in turn were watching the field, waiting for us to make a fatal mistake. As the minutes dragged by some of the younger enemy troops moved out from behind the tanks to the side, facing us, grinning. What a shot! They were less than a hundred yards away and I could have shot the eyes out of any one of them. But not now, not with so many of them and all those tanks sitting right there.

Benson returned and told Brininstool that Lieutenant Sweeny had ordered us to withdraw back inside the town to the windmill. We would make a stand there. Brininstool gave the command for everyone to fall back, a few at a time. It was every man for himself.

Speer took off first, I followed, then Bielski, Phillips, and the others. We slipped carefully out of our holes and began crawling slowly along the rows of tall plants, not wanting to touch them. Doing so would make them move, giving away our positions and bringing fire down on us.

Some of the plants must have moved, though, for the tanks began firing their machine guns. The enemy troops joined in, firing their rifles first at moving tobacco plants and then again wherever. A couple of troopers to our right rose up running and were cut down by small-arms fire. I could hear the impact of the bullets hitting their bodies. The rest of us crawled all the way back to where the tobacco field ended. We were in an apple orchard where the ground was exposed. At that point everyone took off running like a covey of quail flushed by a hunter. The tanks opened up with their cannons, and 75mm and 88mm high-velocity, flat-trajectory shells screamed past us. Machine-gun and rifle bullets cracked around us as we ran. One shell struck a tree near the roots just to my right, splitting the tree in half from its roots to the limb crotch and blowing it completely free of the ground. Other trees were being blown apart, their limbs, huge splinters, and shrapnel flying out among us.

A small trooper carrying a machine gun was struck by shrapnel and went down, dead. I ran back, picked up the machine gun, and gave my rifle to Luke Easly to carry. We both took off running. Lieutenant Rutan, the 1st Platoon leader, was seriously wounded off to our left and went down. Woolf was hit in the belly. Blood flowed freely from a gaping wound. Four men grabbed his arms and legs and ran with him facedown between them. All of A Company and others were in full flight back toward Opheusden, where we could make a stand against the tanks and infantry.

Heavy barbed wire was strung throughout the apple orchard and some men became entangled in it. Others stopped long enough to aid them in getting free. At the end of the orchard was a sparse wood. We continued on until a large group of us came to the edge of the wood. There we encountered a wide, deep ditch running parallel to the road fronting Opheusden. The ditch was filled with a black, foul-smelling sludge.

Men were lowering themselves down a steep bank into the nox-ious mess and making their way waist deep to the steep bank on the opposite side. Many were carrying wounded and men pitched in to help them get their burdens to the other side, keeping the wounded men's bodies out of the muck, then helping them up the bank. I hes-itated, looking at the black ooze in the ditch. Every toilet in Opheus-den probably emptied into the ditch. I knew that with the weight of my pack and the forty-two-pound machine gun I was carrying I would probably sink further into the disgusting morass than the others around me. More shells struck nearby and several tank rounds rifled between us, striking houses in the city itself. The enemy evidently was following hard on our heels. The tanks and infantry were closing in. There was no choice. I slid down into the stinking mess, waded across the thick, heavy, foul-smelling corruption to the other side, and scaled the steep, slimy bank, all the while struggling to hold the ma-chine gun up out of the mess. It was our life at stake.

After finally gaining the road we made our way across and back to the windmill. Because of its high visibility, it soon became the gath-ering point for all the troopers streaming back from the fields west of town. They all came in covered with stinking black slime, some wounded, others helping or carrying the seriously wounded. We all gathered at the windmill. I was standing in front of the open door when the four men carrying Woolf finally carried him in. Blood was still streaming from his belly. *He's dead, got to be dead,* I thought, *or he will be before long.* No one can lose that much blood and live.

Woolf lifted his head, looked straight at me, and said, "Hey, Bur-gett, you mammy crammer, give me a hand."

That was his way—he always spoke in that manner. Even though I was carrying the machine gun, I helped to carry him inside. The interior looked like a slaughterhouse. It was full of wounded, dead, and dying men. One of our surgeons was standing just inside the door opening when a shell hit nearby. A large shell fragment struck the doctor in the belly, disemboweling him. The medics laid the doctor with the other casualties and began covering his wounds with wet gauze. The doctor had lost about twenty feet of gut. I don't know if he made it or not. Several men kept going through the crush of bodies and carried those they thought were dead outside and placed them on the ever-growing dead pile.

Many of the wounded were from the British DCLI, the battalion of stalwart heroes that had attacked through the open field alongside of us. There were just thirty of them left standing of the three hundred that began the attack. No one can ever doubt or question their courage. Those men were soldiers. Their major was heard to say, "It was a bloody good show while it lasted." The son of a bitch should have been out front leading them.

All the while shells continued to land all around us, many of them aimed at the windmill, which was the highest target around. I made my way to the rear of the windmill and moved past the dead pile to where I could see back across the road from which we had come. Stragglers were still making their way in. Benson was there with our other men, covered to his waist with the same muck. As I stood there looking at him it suddenly dawned on me that when he had gone to get permission for us to withdraw he was not gone long enough to get to the windmill and back. Nor had he come back covered with the muck that clung to him now. Benson had not gone all the way back. He had not contacted Lieutenant Sweeny. He had taken it upon himself to tell Sergeant Brininstool that the lieutenant had given the order for us to withdraw. Benson, sizing up the situation and taking it upon himself to take action, had pulled us out of harm's way and probably saved our company from being wiped out. That was my secret. I didn't even let Benson know that I was aware of what had transpired.

"Where's the tripod for this gun?" I called. No one knew. The man carrying it probably was killed or wounded and the damned thing was still out there somewhere.

Justo Correa looked up from where he was sitting near me and pushed a large piece of concrete to me that had been blasted from the windmill. "Here," he said, "it's not a tripod but it's better than nothing."

I placed the machine gun on it and four troopers handed over four boxes of machine-gun ammo they had been carrying. I quickly loaded the gun. Speer, Bielski, Phillips, and several others showed up. Ski was not among our group. I guessed that he had bought the farm. I never saw or heard of him again. Luke Easly showed up next.

"Where's my rifle?" I asked.

"I don't know," he replied. "I haven't got it."

I cursed. That keyhole had lost my rifle. What the hell was I going to do without a rifle? Besides the machine gun I still had my .45, but I felt naked without my rifle.

Flat-trajectory, high-velocity shells suddenly rifled in, fired point-blank from tanks that had approached stealthily on the other side of the ditch. The tanks did not fire directly at the windmill; they knew there were many wounded Germans among our own wounded. The ditch acted as a natural tank barrier. It was too wide and deep for them to traverse, and they were forced to stop at its edge. German infantry came running forward, passing behind and around the tanks. We could see them approaching. Many were very young. Even covered with the grime of battle we could see their boyish features. They looked to be as young as twelve or fourteen. They must have thought we were done, for they were hurrying forward with the overzealous youthful desire to be in on the kill.

Troopers up and down the line opened fire, cutting the young lions down in their tracks. Those who weren't hit quickly dove for cover. I opened up with the machine gun at the same time, slamming long bursts into the enemy side of the ditch. I saw several men go down, hit by my tracers. The damned machine gun kept bouncing around on the piece of concrete and I struggled to hold it down with my left hand while squeezing off bursts with my right. Correa rolled over to me to help with the loading and to feed the belt into the gun. The sound of rifle and machine-gun fire grew to a steady roar. The Germans had gone to ground but still our fire lanced into their positions.

We could see more enemy troops coming forward from their rear. They were bunching up, their lead troops slowed by the wide, stinking ditch. Our small-arms fire lanced into them while our mortars coughed shells into the cluster of men forming on the other side of the ditch. I fired in short bursts, watching my tracers to see where I was hitting and struggling to keep the bucking machine gun as steady as possible. Someone had called for artillery, and shells began pounding the enemy positions. The incoming fire began to slow, then it stopped. The German infantry began to withdraw and their tanks quit firing and backed away out of sight, although we knew they were still out there. Our own artillery came to a halt. Firing was still going on but the volume was nowhere near what it had been.

With things quieted down, troopers took time to consolidate their positions and to scrape together better protection from the piles of bricks, stones, and whatever in front of each man. There wasn't time to dig in. Correa and I had just lain back against the wall to take a breather when Phillips called out, "Hey! There's a trooper over there with something to eat."

We looked over and saw a man coming out the back of a house eating from a glass jar. Several other troopers were also sitting with their backs against the wall of the house eating from glass jars.

"What have you got?" Phillips yelled.

"Cherries," the man replied. "There's a whole bunch of jars in the basement."

Another, smaller drainage ditch ran between the windmill and the houses that the other troopers were eating behind. It ran from the town to the large ditch we had just crossed. A wooden plank had been placed across it as a bridge between the windmill and the houses.

"You men want some cherries?" Correa asked.

"Yeah!" we chorused.

Correa stood up, put his head down, and ran full tilt toward the wooden plank. Halfway across a German machine gun opened up on him. The plank bounced like a springboard but he kept going. I returned fire with my machine gun in the direction of the enemy gun. It quit for the moment.

A few minutes later Correa returned from the basement with his rifle in hand and an armload of cherry jars. He lowered his head and pounded back toward us. I fired long bursts of fire at the German machine gunner but he fired at Correa anyway as he crossed the plank. Then Correa got out of sync with the bouncing plank. His foot was coming down as the plank was going up and he lost his stride and did a fancy little dance with machine-gun bullets lancing all around him before regaining his balance and step.

"Don't drop the cherries," everyone chorused. "Don't drop the cherries."

Correa made it back unscathed and passed around the jars of cherries.

Men were milling about and officers began calling out orders. Noncoms repeated them and soon squads, platoons, and companies began to form—not out in the open but under cover from enemy fire. Slowly order grew out of the chaos. A Company was assigned the right flank of a new perimeter. Lieutenant Muir was no longer with us. He had been badly wounded. The 2d Platoon moved out anyway. I don't know for sure who took command of our platoon at that time. Perhaps it was Sgt. Royce Stringfellow. Sergeant Vetland, our platoon sergeant and second in command, had been wounded by the grenade the dying German prisoners had insisted they didn't throw. The next in line was Sergeant Stringfellow, who was senior to our squad leader, Sergeant Brininstool.

We made our way through the streets under small-arms fire and falling shells, to take up positions along a narrow road leading into town. The houses there were built close together, and there was an empty pigsty to our right.

I set the machine gun up on a rock to give support to a 57mm antitank gun that was set up in the center of the narrow street, facing the enemy. Our squad spread out to the right and left of me seeking places of protection in and around the houses to defend from. Phillips was with me as assistant gunner, and a lone gunner manned the 57mm gun. The rest of his crew had all been killed or wounded. We talked awhile with the gunner, trying to assess our situation and get a feel for what was happening. The trooper on the 57mm gun said he was going to give it his best. We assured him we would do the same.

Suddenly we heard the sound of a tank engine. The gunner hunkered down behind his 57mm gun and I got on the machine gun, Phillips beside me. The sound grew louder. A huge Tiger tank rounded the corner and tried to enter the narrow street. The tank was wider than the narrow street! He kept trying, breaking bricks and stone off the corners of the houses on either side of the street. The 57mm gunner fired head on into the armored monster but the shell just bounced off.

The tank hesitated, then backed up a little. Its large 88mm gun swiveled our way. I grabbed the machine gun and Phillips and I leaped headfirst over the low stone wall running the length of the pigsty and landed in a thick layer of pig mess. That wasn't so bad after our trip across the stinking ditch. The tank's long barrel depressed and we saw the 57mm gunner working at the breech of his gun. We yelled for him to leave the gun and get the hell behind the wall with us. He had pulled the firing pin from the breech and held it in his hand as he leaped over the wall to join us in the pig mess. The Tiger fired its big main gun and the 57mm antitank gun blew all to hell, scattering pieces all over the road.

"What the hell were you doing?" Phillips asked. "You almost got yourself killed."

"I had to get the firing pin," the gunner replied. He said all gunners were instructed that if they ever had to leave their gun for any reason, they were to pull the firing pin and take it with them. That would deny the enemy the use of the gun if it fell into their hands. At the same time, if the gunner ran into another gun without a crew or firing pin, he could put it back into service with his firing pin. He clutched it as though it were made of gold. "It's all I've got," he said. "My gun is gone."

The big tank saw he could not possibly enter the town on this street, so he backed up a little farther and began shelling the buildings behind us and rifled shells at random down the street into town. Slate shingles, knocked loose by the shelling, clattered down the slope of the roof and dropped in front of us as we hunkered underneath an overhanging lean-to.

Finally the tank moved on, probably in search of another way into town or giving up on getting any farther into town altogether. Most tanks would not have entered the narrow streets even if they could. They knew they ran the risk of being trapped there by troops wedging rocks or timbers between their bogie wheels and then setting them afire. The large, open sewer ditch had slowed the enemy tanks from coming directly down on us but they had found their way around and somehow had gotten into town in force, backed by infantry. The narrow streets in this part of town stopped the larger tanks from invading altogether, and we slowed their infantry with small arms and mortars. Our artillery finished the job.

As soon as the tank left, Phillips and I crawled back over the low stone wall and continued to fire the machine gun. However, it bounced around so much on the rock that it wasn't much good for anything over a hundred yards, just a lot of spraying. I did okay with it at close range, though, firing in short bursts and watching the strike of the tracers.

Our command again called for artillery support, which came in from our 321st PFA and the British "Long Tom" 155s. The attack broke up and the Germans withdrew for good. We had held off their biggest assault yet on The Island.

The Germans we stopped were the same ones as the day before: the 363d Volksgrenadier Division reinforced with a battalion of engineers, a regiment of artillery, and an armored division. The 363d Volksgrenadier Division and its attached units were in ruins. It had nearly destroyed itself in numerous attacks against us, only to be outshot, outfought, and decimated by us and our supporting American and British artillery.

Our company was down to less than 30 percent of our original strength. Bodies of men from both sides covered the ground in and around Opheusden. Terrible battles had raged here. Allied statistics recorded that the Germans threw more artillery at us during this battle than they had in any sector since the battle of El Alamein in North Africa.

There wasn't a company left in the 506th PIR's 1st Battalion larger than a normal-sized platoon. The Germans faired much worse. Their 957th Regiment had been completely destroyed in the battles against us on October 5. The next day they sent their 958th Regiment and attached units against us, and they too were destroyed.

The British artillery and Typhoon fighter-bombers played a major role in the destruction of the enemy trying to smash through the narrow corridor between the Waal River and the Neder Rijn in an all-out drive to Nijmegen and the bridge there.

As we readied to withdraw from Opheusden we still had 120 seriously wounded men in our aid station and hidden in the basements of nearby homes. Riflemen from our 1st Battalion were called off the line to help move out the wounded. About fifty of the walking wounded left under their own power that afternoon despite being in great pain. As soon as it grew dark, Maj. Louis R. Kent, the regimental surgeon, obtained several jeeps and an ambulance with which he removed about twenty litter patients along the Neder Rijn dike. The Germans had cut all the other roads. Six more wounded were carried out by German prisoners on litters. Our riflemen carried out the rest using their rifles as a seat, two men to a patient. Machine-gun and mortar crews along with a few riflemen stayed in place on the line. The project took all afternoon and well into the night, with all traveling along the same route.

An hour after the last of the wounded left, around 2 A.M., the 506th PIR formed up in total darkness and moved out in combat formation along the narrow roads, heading back toward the small village of Tuinhoff, a little more than halfway between Opheusden and Zetten.

Our 1st Battalion formed up last. Colonel Sink, the regimental commander, ordered Lieutenant Sweeny, still in command of A Company, to leave a few men behind to serve as a rear guard after the rest of the regiment moved out. These few men were to stay in place and stall the enemy if they launched an attack before the regiment reached its destination and dug in. Lieutenant Sweeny chose Lieutenant Borrelli to head this detail, and he in turn chose Phillips, Bielski, Speer, and me to stay with him—five men to serve as rear guard for an entire regiment. Later reports record in error that a platoon was left behind as rear guard. We were given two .30-caliber machine guns and four boxes of ammo for each gun, plus some extra grenades.

Four men with one officer, two machine guns, and a total of eight boxes of ammo to face a division of infantry, a regiment of artillery, a battalion of engineers, and an armored division. If we were attacked in force the enemy would overrun us in short order but we would at least delay them for a few minutes. And the sounds of battle would alert the rest of the regiment that the enemy was on the way. Those few minutes would give the regiment time to prepare a hasty defense and dig in. If they heard no gunfire they would assume the enemy was still holding in place. We were given permission to pull out and follow the regiment at first light.

We set up our machine guns on a high elevation not too far apart. There was no sense spreading out; we needed to be close enough to cover each other. Lieutenant Borrelli chose a position from which he could observe everything to our front while comfortably seated. We sat quietly, dutifully at our machine guns as the last of the 506th PIR moved out, walking down the road with the thirty remaining British troopers from the DCLI. We watched their vague shadows until they melted into the dark. We listened as the footfalls of boots on the blacktop faded in the distance. We strained to hear the muted metallic sounds of machine guns and mortars being shifted from shoulder to shoulder. At last all was quiet. The entire regiment had pulled out from the battlefront and we, four men and an officer, remained to hold the line alone.

8

The Battle of the Apple Orchard

It very rarely happens in combat but once in a great while it does, especially after a particularly tough battle. It becomes quiet. No artillery barrages, no Screaming Meemies, no mortars, no machine guns, and no rifles being fired. It was quiet. It was so quiet I thought I could hear my own heartbeat. The silence gave way to a ringing in my ears that grew increasingly louder. We didn't even talk to each other for fear the enemy would hear us whispering.

After sitting there in silence for a long time, someone, I don't recall who, began to talk. Soon we were all talking in hushed tones, except for Lieutenant Borrelli. He just sat there cleaning his fingernails with a small knife, listening. We didn't like this quiet. With no enemy artillery coming in we knew the enemy must have patrols out in our territory. No army shells areas where it has patrols working. They would kill their own men. No incoming artillery meant there must be enemy patrols out. That was all we needed: a patrol to come in and discover there were only five men on the entire front line. We would have the whole German army down on us in a heartbeat.

We quickly grew tired of whispering and lay quietly behind our guns, staring out into a dark no-man's-land, looking for a moving shadow, listening for a sound, and praying for the discomforting stillness to remain. We didn't like the quiet but we certainly did not want artillery coming down on us, tanks clanking forward, or enemy troops moving in for the kill, either. Those were sounds we could definitely do without.

Speer slipped through the night quietly to me and said that he saw something over to our far left. Speer had the eyes of a cat. Phillips and I moved over to their gun. Bielski was still watching. We eased in beside him and he pointed without speaking. Phillips and I looked and saw the shadow of a man moving up and over our high ground, heading to what would be our rear. He was followed by another and another and another. It was an enemy patrol out searching for our positions. We sat there motionless, watching the shadows go by.

Minutes after they had melted into the dark we discussed it among the four of us. We would have to be especially alert now. The patrol was behind us, and there would probably be no more patrols directly out in front, so we had to watch our rear carefully for the return of the one patrol. It might come back to our right, to our left, or perhaps right into us. Our lives depended on our seeing or hearing them first when they returned. We had to watch in all directions now. We knew there had to be more patrols out along the entire front but we had seen the one in our area and had watched it pass.

Time went on and we saw no more of the enemy patrol. As the sky began to lighten I moved over toward the lieutenant.

"Hey, Lieutenant Borrelli," I whispered. "When are we gonna move out?"

"We've got plenty of time," he replied. "We'll go when I say so."

That was all there was to it. No sense asking again. The lieutenant would let us know when he was ready to move out.

It was getting pretty light. If we didn't move out soon we would be walking down the streets in broad daylight, visible to every damned German in Holland. After letting us sweat it out for a few more minutes Lieutenant Borrelli said, "Okay, saddle up. Let's go; we're moving out."

Those were the best words we had heard in many days. We quietly pulled our machine guns down from the embankment, divided up the load of machine guns, tripods, and ammo among us, fell in behind the lieutenant, who carried a carbine, and set off down the road.

"Do you know where we're supposed to go, Sir?" I asked.

"Yes, I do," Borrelli replied.

"Is it a secret or will you tell us?" I questioned.

"I'll let you know when we get there," he said.

We walked for what seemed about two miles and I asked, "Are you *sure* you know where we are? We aren't lost are we?"

"Yes, I know where we are, and no, we aren't lost," the lieutenant answered.

I fell back with the others. I didn't like it. Lieutenant Borrelli supposedly knew where we were and where we were going but we didn't. The worst thing was that he wouldn't tell us. We didn't know where the regiment had gone. I have seen officers killed instantly with a bullet through the brain. If this happened to Borrelli we would be screwed. He should have briefed us all thoroughly. Each one of us should have known where we were going. I didn't like having my fate in the hands of just one man. I liked Lieutenant Borrelli very much; we had always gotten along, but I didn't like the way he was handling this detail.

We continued walking along the narrow, lonely road. There was some sort of large ditch or small canal to our immediate left and trees grew along both sides of the road. We passed a small bridge over the waterway on our left. Still we walked. Then we came to an apple orchard. There were troops camped among the trees near the road, some with pup tents set up. It seemed to us they were just getting up. It was about 5:30 A.M. We could have used some sleep ourselves. Some of the troops in the orchard waved to us. We waved back. They weren't paratroopers, so we figured they must be British as we passed on by.

More troops were camped in the same orchard a little farther ahead. They were set up farther back from the road, but we were able to recognize some of them. They were men from our outfit. We went on to where a narrow road came in from the right and butted into the road we were on at the far end of the orchard. We turned onto the road and saw a few houses off to our left. Lieutenant Borrelli said he had to report to the company CP and told us we were on our own. We found the rest of A Company and joined up with our men. After we turned our machine guns back over to the gunners we had borrowed them from I was left with nothing but my .45-caliber pistol. I felt naked without my M1 rifle.

Bielski took over 2d Squad's machine gun, which I had carried back during our withdrawal through the tobacco field the day before. Someone had found a tripod for it, making it a whole gun again. I never did care for the front-mounted bipod; there wasn't enough traverse.

Bielski, Speer, Phillips, and I walked deeper into the trees to where we could look over a field in sort of an inside corner of the orchard. I picked a spot near Benson and began digging. As soon as I got my hole dug, I was going to get some sleep. Bielski moved to where he had a better field of fire for his gun. Speer and Phillips were digging in a little farther off to my left rear. The men who had arrived ahead of us had already finished their holes and were busy attending to their weapons.

Out in the field stood a haystack and an old hand-operated water pump. Men were going over to the pump to fill their canteens, then to the haystack to get an armload of hay for their foxholes. The English camped at the other part of the orchard were doing the same thing. It just so happened that no one from the two different camps chanced to go for water or hay at the same time.

I had dug my hole down about a foot or so when I heard someone yell at the top of his voice, "They're Krauts!" Shots rang out, a couple at first, then a machine gun opened up, then a full-scale shoot-out erupted.

More machine guns opened up as 60mm mortars began to fire. The "English" troops at the other end of the orchard were Germans! More German troops appeared to our far left, running to join the battle. There looked to be a battalion of them. Sergeant Brininstool grabbed the machine gun he had been carrying, picked it up, turned toward the enemy, slammed the gun down, and began firing. All of the troopers and Germans were now firing at each other. The sound was deafening. I could see Germans running through the apple trees and pulled out my .45. I drew a bead on a running enemy, led him a little bit, and squeezed the trigger. The man kept running. Again and again I fired at different Germans but not once did one fall. Damn, what I would have given for my M1 rifle right then. Damn Luke Easly.

More Germans poured in from our left. Our machine guns fired in long bursts, almost without letup. Several of the 60mm mortars to our right front joined in, firing at concentrations of enemy. Riflemen were firing, reloading, and firing again and again. At that moment the man in front of me, who was lying on top of the ground behind a tree, was hit in the head. I literally saw his head explode. Brains flew all over my face and arms. I tried to brush them off the best I could, then I crawled forward and grabbed his rifle.

Back in my foot-deep hole I quickly opened the bolt, checked the bore, reloaded, and aimed at a German as he rose to run toward us. I squeezed off a shot and he went down hard. Now *I* was in the fight, too. Mortar shells continued to slam down on the Germans as two of our platoons moved around their right and left flanks. The enemy coming in from our left slowed their advance. They were confused. Our fire was cutting them down. Captain Warren, the battalion surgeon, walked out into the field between the two warring groups and the firing slowed. Captain Warren walked into the German lines and just stood there. He was the victor and they were the vanquished. The Germans, seeing an American officer standing in their midst, threw down their weapons and began shouting, *"Kamerad! Kamerad!"*

All of our firing stopped except for one machine gun that kept firing. Everyone yelled for the gunner to stop firing so we could end this thing, but he continued to shoot. An older veteran ran over and threatened to kill him as he pulled the man forcibly away from the gun. The man kept yelling over and over, "They're Krauts, damn it! They're Krauts!" I believe he'd had about enough of war.

Gradually the enemy troops got up and came forward, hands held high. A few at first, then more and more. I think some were waiting to see if the first ones would be shot down. When the first ones to surrender made it over to us without being killed, the rest came in. Finally we had them all. We marched them out to the macadam road, turned right on the macadam for a short way, and then onto the dirt road Lieutenant Borrelli and our detail had taken when we arrived. We stood them in a military formation. It was a battalion of Germans, including their commander. The commander asked for some of our aidmen to go back to the field with his aidmen and retrieve his wounded. Permission was granted and several troopers helped the

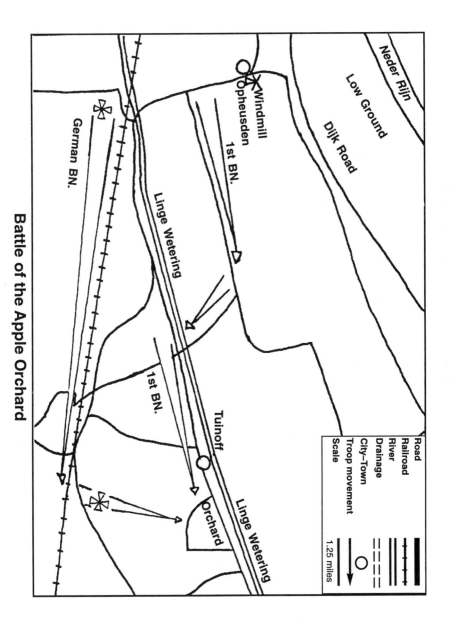

Battle of the Apple Orchard

Germans to bring in their casualties, placing them on the grass in the front yards of the houses.

Our medics began examining them and giving what aid they could. I went to help and talked some with their commander, who was more concerned for his wounded than losing a battle.

"Many wars are fought, won, and lost," he said, "but men die only once."

One wounded man didn't want to take the sulfadiazene tablet a medic had given him after bandaging his wound. The German stood holding the tablet between his thumb and forefinger staring at it.

"For Christ's sake," I said, "take the damned thing! That's the same stuff we take. If we wanted you dead we'd just shoot you." He looked startled, put it in his mouth, and swallowed. I gave him some water from my canteen to wash it down.

More and more of our troopers came to see the prisoners. No one attempted to loot or harass them. In fact, most of our men were trying to help them. I have seen times when these same men were like snarling dogs, wanting to kill everyone and everything, even prisoners. What controls the mood of men?

Several of the Germans who had been camped in the orchard told us they had seen us walk by on the road and waved to us. They knew we were Americans but thought we were prisoners. The German commander admitted that he really didn't know for sure just where he was. He had been given orders and a map and told to go on through to Nijmegen. Somehow he had become disoriented. When he heard the firing and saw that we were killing Germans, he rushed to their aid. Now he and his men were all prisoners.

At that very moment there came a deep vibrating sound that could be felt in the air itself. At first we didn't know what it was. The sound grew louder and we looked up and saw hundreds of our bombers flying low overhead, wingtip to wingtip, stretching side to side from horizon to horizon, with the lead planes passing out of sight over the forward horizon while still more came up from the rear. They were all heading toward Germany.

Our prisoners stared skyward in disbelief. It was an awe-inspiring sight, even to us. American bombers flying wingtip to wingtip, filling the whole sky, and so low in altitude that we could make out the insignia on their wings and fuselages. The Germans stood shaking their heads. *"Alles kaput, alles kaput,"* they repeated over and over. *"Deutschland ist kaput."*

The hour-long "Battle of the Apple Orchard" resulted in approximately 60 Germans dead, about 30 more wounded, and a total of 231 prisoners, including a battalion commander. Our battalion lost 2 killed and 5 wounded. A Company suffered no casualties in the battle. The dead trooper from whom I retrieved the rifle was not in our company.

We used our walking wounded as guards. After turning the Germans over to them we went back to our positions in the apple orchard. Some of our men walked over to the German campsite to loot. The most they came away with was some metal camp mirrors, several backpacks, and a few pistols, nothing we hadn't already seen in large quantities all the way from Normandy.

When the 506th PIR retired from Opheusden, the 327th Glider Infantry from our division set up a new MLR about twelve hundred yards east of that city. The Germans pulled back about a thousand yards west of the city, leaving a broad no-man's-land through which they continued to attack the 327th Regiment with what was left of the 363d Volksgrenadier Division. The attacks led to the final and total destruction of the 363d Division in some of the most brutal battles of the war. Hand-to-hand fights were common, with many men being killed with knife and pistol. After several such battles in the dark of night, daylight revealed German bodies within arm's reach of many of the 327th's foxholes and machine-gun emplacements.

An example of the grim nature of the battles that took place in Opheusden during our stay and the stay of the 327th was told to me by a resident of Opheusden fifty-four years after the war ended during one of my return trips to the battle sites.

The man was eleven years old at the time and remembers well hiding in the family cellar while the battle raged above. American paratroopers and Germans were intermixed within the city, fighting as they ran into each other. He said he was hiding in a corner of the cellar with his parents when two paratroopers entered the house above. One of them sat down at the large piano in the parlor and began playing classical music. Who knows why? Perhaps it was a release from the war. His buddy, a very large man, leaned against the wall listening to the music.

Two Germans appeared from between the houses across the street and stopped and listened. Where was the music coming from and why? One of them stepped forward, slowly approached the house, cautiously opened the front door, and stuck his head inside.

It wasn't planned that way, but the large trooper grabbed the German, yanked him through the door, cut his throat, and threw his body in a corner. The German waiting on the other side of the road, wondering why his comrade had stayed in the house so long, wandered across the street and stuck his head inside. The big trooper grabbed him, jerked him into the room, slashed his throat, and dumped him in the corner on top of his dead comrade. It became a game, the one trooper playing classical music to lure the Germans in, the other cutting their throats. In the end there were eleven German bodies stacked in the corner.

This Dutch citizen, who still resides in Opheusden and who bought me a fish dinner while he told me his story, said his family was too frightened to move, even when the blood began to soak through the floor above and drip down on them. He was very serious as he related the story. I cannot verify that it really happened; I just relate it here as he told it to me.

9
On the Rhine

We left the prisoners we took during the Battle of the Apple Orchard, along with their wounded, with our walking wounded and returned to our positions and began digging again. Dig a hole. That was the first thing we always did, whether taking a long break during a march or moving into a position. As soon as we stopped, everyone began digging a hole—either a slit trench or a foxhole. If artillery came in or an attack started without warning, those without a hole had nowhere to take cover and many died on the spot. I preferred a square or round foxhole to the slit trench. It offered less open space overhead for shell fragments to enter, and better protection if overrun by tanks.

About the time I completed the hole and stood wiping the sweat from my face, we were ordered to form up. We were moving out. That was the way it always seemed to be. As soon as you finished digging a hole it was time to move out. On marches where we stopped from five to ten times while en route we dug that many holes—or at least started to. I don't know how many holes I dug in my combat career.

We put our gear on, shouldered our weapons, distributed our crew-served weapons and extra ammo, and headed out. Shrapnel was still with the outfit, running up and down our ranks as we marched. He had adopted A Company, and the men of A Company—as GIs always do—took care of him. He was already getting fat from the scraps everyone fed to him.

The sounds we heard were of our rubber-soled boots on the narrow blacktop road, the metallic clanks of our heavy weapons being shifted from shoulder to shoulder or passed from man to man, and the creaking of harnesses and rifle slings. No one talked much, especially Lieutenant Borrelli, Phillips, Bielski, Speer, and me. We had been without sleep for nearly three days now, including all of the previous night while we were on rear guard. Most of the men in the regiment had gotten at least three hours of sleep after they arrived in the apple orchard. We five didn't because the shooting started within minutes after our arrival.

We marched without incident back to our old bivouac site in the Zetten-Andelst area. There we set up in a defensive position and dug in. They issued us more English rations—this time I got bully beef—and we brewed compo tea. We had been on English rations since arriving on The Island and really weren't too happy with them. We would rather have had a good cup of coffee than that compo tea. I finished my rations and dozed off in my hole.

While conducting patrols, men of the 506th PIR discovered a large jam factory in German territory in Dodewaard when we first arrived. It was stocked from end to end with jars of jam. All hours of the day or night one could see troopers sneaking into no-man's-land and then come staggering away from the jam factory with one or more cases of jam. Everyone on The Island used jam at every meal. In between we had jam on nearly everything we ate, including the English biscuits. After a while we even tried it on bully beef—but *never* the oxtail soup.

October 8, 1944. We spent the entire day cleaning and recleaning our weapons, sharpening our trench knives, scraping crud from clothing, and trying to look like soldiers again. Some men took a "whore's bath," washing their faces, armpits, and crotches with cold water from a helmet. We always washed our feet last, taking one boot off at a time and washing that foot, putting the boot back on, then doing the same with the other foot. If an attack started or an artillery barrage came in, you didn't want to have to be running around barefoot. That was why we always washed our feet one at a time, keeping the boot we'd taken off handy. Our boots were soggy, wet from the constant rain of the past two weeks and the water in the bottoms of our holes. One could not dig two feet anywhere in Holland without striking water.

On October 9, Capt. R. P. Meason transferred into A Company as our new commander, and Lieutenant Sweeny assumed command of our 2d Platoon. One of the first things Lieutenant Sweeny did was to hold an inspection. We were given advance notice of the inspection and cleaned everything as best we could, especially our weapons. We lined up, dressed right, and stood at attention. Lieutenant Sweeny walked out in front of us, looked us over, and asked, "Is this all there is?"

"Yes, Sir," Sergeant Brininstool replied. "Fifteen men, Sir."

That was it, three squads of five men each. Second Platoon was little more than a normal-size squad. The other platoons in A Company hadn't fared any better. We looked up and down our short ranks and began laughing.

"This is it, Lieutenant," someone said. "This is it."

Lieutenant Sweeny called us back to attention and walked up and down our ranks, inspecting our clean weapons and our cruddy persons. He complimented us on our fine condition and dismissed us.

From October 10 through 19 there was no change in our status and nothing much happened. We just stayed where we were, soaked to the skin by the almost daily rains. Whenever possible we got out of our foxholes, which were half filled with water. During our stay there we could hear German V-2 rockets being launched almost daily against targets in England. These huge rockets carried a one-ton high-explosive warhead and reached an altitude of sixty miles as they arched through the sky at a speed of thirty-six hundred miles per hour. They plummeted silently down ahead of the sound of their approach, exploding without warning in England's crowded cities. This was even more terrifying to the Brits than the V-1 buzz bomb, which could at least be heard, seen, and shot down. No one heard or saw a V-2 coming in. By the time the sound of its approach caught up to it, it was too late.

It was also there that we saw one of the first combat jet fighters used in war. It was a twin-engine Messerschmitt Me-262, and it came in low and fast, crossing from our right to our left, did a 180-degree turn, and left the same way it had come. The next day at precisely the same time it came again. The British fired on it with antiaircraft guns, but the jet was so fast that it was well out of range by the time the first shells exploded in the air overhead. Then, as though taunting the gunners, the pilot flew back over us and headed for home.

The next day the jet came over at the same time again. This time the British had a flight of Spitfires waiting high overhead. When the German jet appeared the Spitfires plummeted straight down, bent on shooting him out of the sky. Hermann the German blew past the English fighters as they approached the spot where they had planned on shooting him down. The Spitfires bottomed out and had just begun to climb when the Messerschmitt completed its turn and roared right over the English fighters. Again the German was gone.

This game went on for several days. Finally the English gave up and ignored the jet on its daily flights. We would stand near our foxholes just to see it. The German jet came and went as it pleased.

These German weapons inspired a new generation of weapons we take for granted today. The V-1 buzz bomb was, in fact, the first cruise missile; the V-2 rocket was the first successful ballistic missile; and the Me-262 was the first jet fighter plane to engage in air combat successfully. Germany in this short period opened the door and dragged the entire world into a new era of warfare.

Our vacation ended on October 20. We were ordered to saddle up and head out to a new line. We were to march to Randwijk, a little town on the Neder Rijn between Opheusden and Hetern. Walking on the blacktop roads wasn't bad, but when we had to cross open fields we were always slipping and sliding in the mud. In some fields the mud would cling to our boots, making it hard to walk. However, that was nothing new; we'd had the same experience all during our training, even in the states.

We arrived in Randwijk that same day, walking down the main street. The Germans were just across the dike on the north bank. Most of them had taken up residence in a brick factory near the Neder Rijn. The place was like a fortress, with piles of bricks stacked all over. British Typhoons had attacked it several times with bombs and rockets without effect. The Germans were there to stay, using the brick factory as a stronghold from which they could run patrols and maintain their lines.

Someone in the outfit that was there before us had set up a German 81mm mortar and stacked about a truckload's worth of shells for it on the road near the base of a brick building. Almost every trooper who passed that way going to and from the chow hall or any other reason would pull the pin on a shell or two and drop them down the tube. Some men would drop three or four rounds down the tube and then watch for them to come down in the ruins of the old brick factory. Every so often a man would turn the traversing screw one way or the other or adjust the elevation to shift the strike of the rounds. It was always possible, and hoped for, that a shell would land on an enemy squad, wiping it out. The mortar had been fired so many times that the base plate had been driven at least four inches down through the blacktop surface of the road.

We set up in houses overlooking the dike and were now somewhat out of the rain most of the time. We also had a change of chow. Our command, knowing how miserable it was to survive on bully beef, oxtail soup (with the bones jelled in tallow), and tea, had made arrangements to have hot meals prepared by the Canadians in our area. We ate in staggered shifts so that men were manning the front lines and outposts at all times. The Canadians set up the mess hall in one of the buildings and served us meals that came close to American cooking, including coffee and fresh-baked bread.

We also had plenty of fresh, clean water available. While in combat and whenever possible we had our drinking water delivered to us. Most of the time the water came in by truck, in jerry cans. When trucking it in wasn't feasible, the Air Corps would send in L-5 artillery spotter aircraft with water. The pilots would fly in low over the front-line troops and tip to one side, dropping several long, sausage-shaped plastic containers filled with water. Sometimes they would miss and we would have to run out into no-man's-land to retrieve the precious liquid, getting shot at in the process. As the plastic containers hit the ground they would bounce, then lie there in the open, waiting to be picked up. Usually one or two would burst, showering water over the already-soaked ground.

On one such drop a plastic container lay about a hundred yards out in front of us in no-man's-land. We needed and wanted that water. It lay there in its clear plastic cocoon, sparkling in the autumn sun, five gallons of fresh, clean water that tantalized us, tempting us to come out and get it. One man darted out but the Germans opened up with rifle fire and he spun around in his tracks and returned to his hole faster than he had left.

"I'll get that damned water!" another trooper shouted. It had become a challenge. He darted out, scooped up the water bag, and, without missing a beat of his running feet, circled back with the water on his shoulder. That was no mean feat. Five gallons weighs about 42.5 pounds. The Germans fired several more shots at him but he got back safely with the water.

Two days after our arrival in Randwijk, A Company was called inside a house to a large rear room that had once served as the kitchen eating area of the Dutch family who had lived there. We were briefed on a mission to be executed that night, October 22–23. The mission called for our 2d Battalion and some Canadian engineers to cross the Neder Rijn in assault boats. Our company would stand guard and act as guides on the south shore. The mission would take place in total darkness, at a time appointed by meteorologists when the moon would not be visible in the sky.

The mission, as it was briefed to us, was to bring back a number of English paratroopers who had been left behind on the enemy side of the river. These men, who had missed the first large evacuation of British 1st Airborne Division troopers left stranded north of the Neder Rijn on September 26, had been secreted in basements and homes by the Dutch at great risk to their own lives.

Using an undetected underwater telephone cable that ran under the Neder Rijn, Dutch partisans had made arrangements to get these men back to the Allied side. For several nights running before the actual date of the mission, a British Bofors antiaircraft gun would fire a long string of tracers out over the river. This was done so the Germans would not become suspicious if the gun were fired in support of the assault crossing for the first time the night of the mission.

Late that evening, men from 2d Battalion carried the assault boats forward from storage places behind our lines and hid them along the base of the dike. Canadian engineers, who were well trained in this sort thing, supervised the handling of the boats.

After dark everyone was in place, waiting for the first signal from farther upstream. Men waited and shivered in the wet cold. There was a heavy mist in the air and a drizzling rain fell steadily through the night. Engineer tape (a durable white cloth tape about two inches wide primarily used to mark cleared pathways through minefields) had been laid down to show the route to be taken by the returning men. The tapes were laid down about a hundred yards from and parallel with the river dike on our side. At regular intervals another tape was joined to the first at a 90-degree angle, leading to shelters in blacked-out bunkers and basements well within the town of Driel.

Batteries of artillery and heavy mortars were aimed to fire around a boxed target area on the river's north bank. This was to be used only if the Germans came upon the men before they could escape onto the river. The artillery and mortars would open up, plastering the far shore all around the area where our men would be, hopefully destroying the Germans.

Our company moved stealthily out of Randwijk, following the roads in total darkness to the very edge of the Neder Rijn. We would serve as guides for the men returning from the far shore and also maintain a firing line with machine guns and mortars set up on the flanks, ready to cover their withdrawal if they were discovered.

I walked with Speer, Correa, Bielski, and Phillips. We made it to the dike with the rest of A Company and waited there, shivering in the cold rain. Upstream came a signal from a red-lens flashlight that was shielded by a long tube and aimed like a rifle in our direction so it could only be seen by looking straight at it. The signal flashed: dot, dot, dot, dash—the Morse code "V for Victory" signal. The Bofors gun fired a long burst of tracers out across the Neder Rijn toward the enemy side as it had done on each of the previous nights. The British paratroopers were to align themselves under the path of the tracers being fired and wait in hiding for our rescue team to arrive.

The Canadian engineers issued commands in hushed tones, lining troopers up on either side of the boats, ordering them to take hold as they had just practiced back in town before coming down to the dike. We watched, fascinated. I wanted to go along. I had spent many hours since childhood in boats and canoes on the waters and marshes of Michigan, and I could tell this was the first time some of these men had been around a small boat.

Silently they dragged the boats up the dike, slid down the other side, and eased their boats quietly into the water. They pulled away slowly, paddling silently, heading for the other side with Canadian engineers sitting in the stern of each boat directing them. They quickly disappeared into the darkness. As promised, there was no moon. The rain clouds helped make it even darker.

We waited there for what seemed to be hours, like expectant fathers in a maternity lounge. I shivered uncontrollably, I think more from excitement than the wet, cold night. A German flare burst high overhead when the boats were about halfway back, and the men in the boats froze, not daring to move. The flare hung in the sky for several long minutes, making a sound like sizzling bacon in a frying pan. A brilliant white light that sputtered and danced illuminated the whole area, causing things to stand out starkly against the black shadows. We turned our heads away and closed our eyes tight so they would adjust to the dark more quickly after the flare went out. It finally burned itself out and total darkness returned; the boats had not been seen. Finally we saw vague shadows on the water. The boats appeared out of the mist and silently beached. We took hold, helping the men ashore.

The 2d Battalion men helped the passengers up forward to disembark while we waded out to our knees to help the men in back over the gunwales and onto shore. As soon as the men were all safely ashore we helped them up the dike and down the other side, leading them to the engineer tape and instructing them to follow it to the right or left until they came to a tape running off at a right angle. They were then to follow that tape to a shelter where they would be fed and warmed.

The British paratroopers were all smiling. They had suffered through an unspeakable hell in their battles against armor and multitudes of enemy foot soldiers, including Waffen SS troops. Then they had been forced to hide under the very noses of the enemy for a nerve-wracking month with the aid and care of the Dutch people. They must have dreaded each scraping footfall, each crunch of gravel outside, the thud of hobnailed boots on floors overhead. The anxiety they felt while hidden in cellars, dugouts, and bunkers by Dutch civilians who faced certain death at the hands of the Germans if they were caught had been barely endurable. If discovered, the paratroopers would have been taken to prisoner of war camps. The civilians would have been shot on the spot—men, women, and children.

These men who had suffered so much, who had fought so well and given a good account of themselves in battle, had lost so many buddies. They looked on us as their saviors, smiling in gratitude and saying over and over, "God bless you, Yank. We'll never forget you."

The credit and thanks did not belong to us, though. It belonged first to the survivors who had the courage and perseverance to withstand what the average person could not. It belonged to the Dutch people, who, faced with the prospect of torture and death, hid and fed them for days on end and who in the end arranged their rescue. It belonged to the men of 2d Battalion, 506th PIR, 101st Airborne Division, who paddled the assault boats across the Neder Rijn into the Germans' front yard and brought the fugitives back right under the enemy's nose. It belonged to the Canadian engineers who brought the boats to where they were needed and gave a crash course to American amateurs on how to navigate across a swift, wide, dangerous river in the black of night. The Canadians unerringly piloted the boats to unseen and unmarked landing points on either side of the river through the swift current and inky-black darkness. The credit goes to all of them. We simply stood there on the shore, praying for them, our airborne brothers. We were ready to fight, yes, but we were the ones who waited.

That dark, moonless night 138 British soldiers, four American pilots, and several Dutch civilians made it safely to our side of the river. Not one shot was fired, other than the signal burst by the Bofors gun. Not one person was wounded. Not one life was lost.

We guided the survivors to the engineer tape and to the cellars where they received hot coffee, biscuits, and jam. We had lots of jam, a factory filled with jam. Later, British troops took over, escorting them to trucks and driving them to Nijmegen for hot showers, fresh clothing, a hot meal, and a real bed. Their nightmare experience would remain with them throughout the rest of their lives. But that night they were alive, a few of the many who dropped on the north bank of the Neder Rijn that fateful day, September 17, 1944.

A little over 10,000 British and Polish paratroopers and glidermen landed in Holland. Their losses at the time of their evacuation were 7,528 killed, wounded, or missing in action. By way of comparison, our 101st Airborne Division, whose roster listed 14,266 men going in, suffered 3,792 casualties, and the 82d Airborne Division reported 3,400 casualties during Operation Market-Garden and subsequent fighting in Holland. There is no exact count of German casualties, but they were high, possibly as many as 15,000.

After the rescue operation we trudged back to Driel along the dark, lonely roads through a lightly falling rain and the chill of night. It didn't matter to us; we all felt higher than a kite. We had helped some of our airborne brothers make it out of that madhouse across the river alive. Arriving back at our places on the line, we again took our posts with our machine guns and mortars. It had been a long, cold night but the memory of those men stepping out of the boats onto friendly soil remains warmly etched in my mind.

10 Attrition

October 24, 1944. We manned our outposts and machine-gun emplacements and cleaned our weapons whenever we were able to get inside a building out of the weather. The mess hall and the Canadian cooking along with real coffee and fresh bread from their bakery made life a little more bearable. We were, however, fully aware that we no longer held the prestige or distinction of being airborne. Field Marshal Montgomery was using us as regular infantry with total disregard for our airborne status, and with no sign of relief in sight.

More than a week before, General Brereton asked Field Marshal Montgomery for the release of all U.S. airborne troops in Holland but got no response. General Brereton repeated his request several more times but was completely and arrogantly ignored each time. General Brereton then wrote to Field Marshal Montgomery, advising him that keeping airborne soldiers in the front lines as infantry violated one of the cardinal rules of airborne employment. Monty continued to ignore General Brereton's requests, keeping the 101st and 82d Airborne Divisions on the front lines, where the number of wounded and dead mounted. At least he saw to it that we were amply backed by British long-range artillery.

Exasperated, General Brereton went over Monty's head and presented his case to General Eisenhower, the supreme commander of all Allied forces in Europe. General Eisenhower knew, as did every lowly private, that Operation Market-Garden had been a total failure. To make matters worse, this senseless war of attrition was bleeding our airborne units to death. The Germans no longer had the

strength to attack southward in force, and the British did not have
the men or resources to make a successful attack across the Neder
Rijn. It was a stalemate; the two armies facing off along the line bleeding each other dry. But Field Marshal Montgomery refused to ac-
knowledge that his plan had failed. He refused to admit defeat. So
it was that the many requests for our release from General Brereton
went unheeded and unanswered.

General Eisenhower finally came to a decision. To keep political
peace in his military family, Monty could continue to use us until the
British cleared the area around Antwerp. As soon as that was accomplished we were to be immediately released from his command
and withdrawn from Holland. In view of Montgomery's past per-
formances, that could take months. But the die was cast and we remained to be used as Monty saw fit.

Almost immediately after Ike's decision was announced, we were
moved up to the dike, closer to Arnhem and the railroad bridge
there. The Germans held both sides of the Neder Rijn, including the
railroad bridge and the Arnhem highway bridge. South of the river
our battle lines were separated by a dike running parallel to the river
with the Germans on the north side of the dike and us on the south.
On the south side of the dike the Allies and German forces were separated by the railroad, which ran south to north over the Neder Rijn,
the Germans on the east side and us on the west side. The junction
of the railroad and dike formed a corner where many bitter and
bloody battles raged between individuals, units, and armor for possession of the area and the south end of the railroad bridge, earn-
ing it the nickname "Coffin Corner."

Again we were put on English rations and ordered to man outposts facing the enemy. Our squad moved into a small house near
the foot of the dike and dug water-filled foxholes in a perimeter
around it. We only used the house to take a cold bath from a helmet
or to get out of the rain if we were not on guard duty. We spent the
rest of the time on alert in our foxholes, watching the dike and the
German-held ground on the other side of the river.

One afternoon Bielski and I were sitting in the back door of the
small house while I washed my socks. Bielski was watching a young
pig eat apples that had fallen from the nearby trees.

"You know," he said, turning toward me, "I sure could go for some young, tender pork right now."

"So could I," I replied, returning his gaze.

We couldn't afford to shoot the pig because the Germans were in the neighborhood on the other side of the dike and the commotion would surely have attracted an unwanted artillery barrage. We also knew it would be all but impossible to run the pig down and bayonet it. Pigs are a lot quicker than they look. So we searched the house for a silent weapon.

"That's it," Bielski announced, pointing to a hand-operated water pump in the back room. The pump had a long, curved, cast-iron handle. We removed the bolts and Bielski hefted it.

"It's just right," he declared.

I went out, gathered some apples, and threw one to the pig, who eyed it warily before moving over to eat it. I threw another, a little closer this time. Again the pig approached cautiously and ate the apple. There must have been something special about the apples I threw because there were hundreds of them lying around. I finally enticed the pig to the door, one apple at a time, and called out, "Hold it Bielski, I'm coming in. The pig is following me."

I stepped well inside the room, rolled an apple just inside the door, and waited, motionless. Bielski stood next to the doorway holding the heavy cast-iron pump handle overhead. The pig was wary but curiosity won out. He stepped inside and bit into the apple. Bielski brought the pump handle down with both hands, crushing its skull. The pig died instantly.

We butchered it and boiled small chunks of pork in our helmets, which we filled with water and set over small fires. Soon men from our platoon came around sniffing the air.

"Whatcha got cookin'?" was the first question everyone asked.

I hadn't counted on the smell of boiling pork traveling so far.

We wound up sharing the pork with the entire platoon. There weren't that many of us left, and the small pig fed us all with some left over. While I was sitting there eating I began to think that the GI helmet was one of the greatest assets a man could have in a combat situation. We took baths from it, washed our dirty underwear and socks in it, dug foxholes with it, used it for a thundermug when it was necessary, bailed water out of our foxholes with it, cooked our meals in it, and wore it for protection.

The next night a truck pulled in next to our outpost to take four of us to man a listening post close to the railroad bridge. Except for one or two men, that was our whole squad, what was left of it. At midnight Bielski, Phillips, Speer, and I boarded the truck and were driven to a lonely spot near the water's edge. One of the men on the truck led the way. We waded through knee-deep water to a small house nearly abutting the dike. Inside we found engineer tape stretching across the room at angles from all the windows.

When one of us asked what the tape was for someone explained that it had been put there to keep men from wandering into that space, which was visible to snipers on the dike. The Germans had dug tunnels through the dike from their side, leaving small apertures on our side from which they could snipe undetected at individuals on this side. Three men had been killed in this house and several Englishmen had been killed in the surrounding area. The British posted their own snipers to look for the German shooters but none had been detected as yet. They were still sniping and killing. Many men have been shot and wounded by ordinary enemy foot soldiers and later claimed it was a sniper who wounded them. They're wrong, though. Snipers don't *wound;* they *kill.*

There was no furniture in the house, no place to sit or lie down, only knee-deep greasy, dirty, sewer water. The Germans had breached the dike enough to let water through and flooded this area. The river water mingled with the putrid sludge in the drainage and sewer ditches that prevailed on The Island, creating a noxious, foul-smelling mess. The four men who had stood guard for the past twenty-four hours explained the setup to us, wished us luck, and left after telling us we would be relieved at midnight the next night.

For hours we stood in the foul water, moving from room to room in the darkness. We could not have a light of any kind, and we did not dare go near the windows. To do either was to invite death. We simply stood in the knee-deep water with our rifles slung on our shoulders for hours on end. Our job, or so we were told, was to listen for unusual noises coming from the other side of the dike. We were to report tank or vehicle movements, talking, the sound of men marching, or anything else we thought suspicious by phone to regimental headquarters. If the enemy had launched a surprise attack, day or night, the four men on that post would have been a sacrifice to be discovered when the next shift arrived the following night.

In time Speer and I became so tired that we started to doze while standing there. We just wanted to lie down and sleep for an hour. The other two could stand guard during that time and then we would spell them. Speer found something large, soft, and soaked—possibly an old couch—in what used to be the kitchen. It was wet, but at least it was above the water level. We took our wallets and cigarettes (Speer didn't smoke), put them in our helmets, eased down into the greasy water, placed our heads on the spongy pillow, and dozed off.

When our buddies woke us up it was early morning. Gray light began to fill the room as we stood up, soaked and chilled. We looked at the "couch" we had been sleeping on and saw that it was the rotting carcass of a dead goat. We were accustomed to dead and rotting corpses being all around us but I didn't like the idea of having snuggled up on a dead goat while I slept.

We spent the whole day walking around in the knee-deep, greasy water in the small areas of the house. We were stuck there until midnight, when our relief would come in total darkness, just as we had, unseen by the snipers. Only then would we be allowed to make our way back to the parked truck that would take us back to our outpost back on the line.

Night finally came, and with it our relief. We briefed the newcomers on the windows and the engineer tape, what to do and what not to do, wished them luck, and left. I wondered later if any of them tried sleeping on the dead goat as Speer and I had.

A day or two later we were informed that each man on The Island would be issued an empty five-gallon jerry can. We were to carry it with us at all times. It seems the Germans gave the British an ultimatum to clear out or they would blow a hole in the dike and flood the entire region. This was no idle threat. They had already done it on a smaller scale, probably to show us that they were serious.

We went a few at a time to where the British had pulled up several six-by-six trucks loaded with empty gas cans. As we filed past the truck with troopers from other units we were handed a can and warned that we would be court-martialed if we lost it, threw it away, or were caught without it at any time. We were further warned that the Germans were going to blow up the dike and flood the surrounding countryside. There were estimates of up to sixteen feet of water that might come in, and our empty gas can was our life flotation device. When the flood came, we were told, hang on to the gas can and swim to the nearest house, barn, or high ground, if there was any.

The British command wasn't about to pull us out and leave The Island to the Germans after all the fighting and casualties it had taken to gain this ground in the first place. We had to stay. The Germans, due to our presence and the continued threat of an Allied attack on Arnhem, figured they would have to blow the dike to be rid of us. It was a standoff, but not for long.

After receiving our cans Phillips, Bielski, Speer, and I walked to one of the English 155mm gun emplacements to socialize with the crew and see what they were doing. They were getting the big gun ready to move out. During our talk they showed us the gun that would be taking its place. It was a wooden electric utility pole set on a wooden carriage. A battery-powered red light was fastened on the "muzzle" end. Only older, worn-out 155mm guns were to be left in place to carry out fire missions. All of the newer artillery pieces were to be moved out at night. When a call for fire did come down, the gun crews would fire the few older guns as fast as possible while flashing the red lights on the dummies. This was supposed to make German observers think full batteries of artillery still remained in place, when in fact only a few junky 155s were all that was left.

I don't recall what day it was, but the Germans were true to their word. They placed a large aerial bomb deep inside the dike near Arnhem and blew a large opening that flooded everything clear back to Opheusden. The blast came without warning. Our squad was caught at our outpost near the dike when the water came. We scrambled to the roof and waited, each man with his gas can at his side. We spent several hours perched like chickens on a roost while watching Canadian engineers with assault boats pick up men from other nearby roofs. The small boats would fill with men, leave, and return for more. We yelled to the Canadians, who assured us our turn was coming. A Canadian in an assault boat who seemed to be getting a big kick out of it finally picked us up. He grinned at us as we clambered aboard. His boat could hold sixteen to twenty men, had a flat bottom, and was powered by a large outboard motor. Curious, I asked about the motor. Being raised as a depression-era kid in Michigan with its nearly twelve thousand lakes, I had spent a lot of time on the water—but always rowing. I had seen only one outboard motor that I could recall. It was owned by a neighbor and was small enough to carry in one hand. The outboard motor on our craft was huge, and I was curious about it.

The Canadian engineer said it was an American-made, fifty-horsepower model that was simply awesome. It stood six feet tall on end and weighed two hundred pounds. From that day on I dreamed of owning one, although I never did.

We were taken to dry land where we assembled with others of our company and battalion. Not all of our division, or even our regiment, was caught in the water. The only ones really affected were the men manning outposts near the dike when the Germans made good their threat.

After that the days flowed one into the other. We were in and out of what were called rest areas at the front, although we were never out of enemy rifle or artillery range. We pulled patrols and stood guard on outposts and listening posts. Time wore on but Field Marshal Montgomery still refused to allow us to leave his command.

On November 11, Armistice Day, the 82d Airborne Division was assembled, boarded trucks, and left the Nijmegen area. British troops took over their old positions.

Two weeks later, while we were in a relatively quiet area eating from American ten-in-one rations, a regiment of Scots came marching up the road near us. They were wearing regular British battle dress, and we could hear their bagpipes screeching noisily as they approached our positions. We heard them while they were still a long way off and ran to the road to watch them go by. The column stopped, and so did the screeching and wailing. With some formality our officers were told that we were officially relieved from duty under Field Marshal Montgomery's command and were under orders to leave.

Canadian trucks pulled up a short time later and we boarded them without any misgivings. Again we traveled over the Nijmegen bridge, this time heading south. After a few miles our convoy pulled onto the grounds of a large monastery. We were ordered inside and told to strip naked, which we did, leaving our weapons on top of our cast-off clothes. We were then moved forty men at a time to a large room where a sergeant told us to get ready for our first shower in seventy-two days. Hot water sprayed from holes drilled in pipes fastened to the ceiling and we began soaping ourselves. They turned off the water so as to conserve hot water for the others, and we scrubbed our bodies for two or three minutes. Then they turned the hot water back on and allowed us another minute or two to rinse off before turning it off again and ordering us out of the shower room.

In the next room we received new socks, underwear, and combat uniforms, and were allowed a few minutes to shave, using one of the many small mirrors fastened around the four walls. We still retained our Class A OD uniforms, which we had worn under our jumpsuits. We put the new combat clothes over the Class A's.

Outside we were ordered to board English lorries and six-by-six trucks with English drivers. Again we headed south through Holland. As we passed through the towns and cities along the way, the Dutch people who saw us would stop whatever they were doing and call out, "September seventeen, September seventeen," all the while holding up their hands with fingers extended in the V for victory sign.

These people hadn't forgotten. They had aided us at every possible opportunity, even to the point of giving their lives. This was their country. The Germans had been there too long. Freedom was on the horizon.

Our convoy moved on through the towns we had fought so hard for: Grave, Uden, Veghel, Koevering, St. Oedenrode, Zon, and Eindhoven. We left the lines in Holland on November 27 and were finally trucked out of the country on November 28, 1944. We had spent seventy-two continuous days on the line in the Netherlands. During that time the 101st Airborne Division sustained 3,792 casualties. Our convoy was headed on a thirty-six-hour road trip to Mourmelon-le-Grand, an old World War I military base in France, bringing an end to our battle for the road to Arnhem.

Epilogue

The road to Arnhem was a difficult one. However, this book would not be complete without a brief account of what happened to our British and Polish airborne brothers assigned to hold the top rung of the ladder extending from Belgium to the Neder Rijn. Their story, like ours, began on D day, September 17, 1944, with its massive jumps and glider landings.

The Red Devils of the British 1st Airborne Division—led by Maj. Gen. Roy Urquhart, who rode in on a glider—dropped and landed on their DZs and LZs near the small towns of Wolfheze and Heelsum, about six to eight miles west and northwest of the Arnhem highway bridge. As with the Americans, several of their gliders were aborted on takeoff, more went down en route, and yet others were either shot down over enemy territory or crashed on the landing zones. Some of their critically needed heavy weapons were lost as a result. The men were well trained and went about the business of assembling in orderly fashion and removing equipment from the gliders that landed safely and recovering what they could from those that had crashed. Many men were also lost as a result of these mishaps.

Airborne forces always suffered losses of men, equipment, and weapons—even in practice maneuvers. In combat, though, the estimates were never correct. At times many men were lost when only a few losses were expected whereas at other times the losses were much lower than expected. But always there were losses. The British troopers quickly closed ranks, with men taking on the priority jobs of those who didn't make it and using whatever equipment and weaponry was on hand to fill in for lost equipment and weapons. The mission must not fail.

Machine guns, mortars, and troops of the 1st Air Landing Brigade dug in around the drop and landing zones to defend against expected enemy attacks and to hold the zones for the air landings that would follow over the next three days. Men of the other brigades formed up in combat formations of companies, platoons, and squads and gathered jeeps, antitank guns, motorcycles, and whatever else they needed.

Major Freddie Gough quickly assembled his small, specialized motorized reconnaissance squadron. Although twenty-two of his gliderborne jeeps, motorcycles, and special weapons had been lost in crashes, he managed to gather up sixty-six heavily armed jeeps and 264 men and struck out on his mission: mounting a surprise attack on the Arnhem bridge, securing the northern end, and holding until the rest of the 1st Parachute Brigade arrived.

Three battalions of airborne foot troops moved out toward Arnhem and the bridge via three different routes, all originating at the drop zones and heading east. A battalion led by Lt. Col. D. Dobie followed Gough's recon squadron on a west-to-east road that lay to the north of Arnhem. Their job was to set up a strong defense line running across the northern end of the city. Another battalion followed the road running toward the center of the city. They were to attack straight onto the bridge from the north, clearing it of all enemy troops. Lieutenant Colonel John D. Frost's battalion went forward on the road that followed alongside the Neder Rijn to the bridge. His men were expected to capture the railroad and pontoon bridges while en route, then aid Gough with the assault and securing of the main bridge.

Confusion and disbelief reigned among the Germans from the commanders to the troops in the field. Was this a maneuver to cut off their retreating Fifteenth Army from Antwerp? Was this an invasion of Holland? Or was this a full-scale effort to drive through the back door into Germany? One of the first to react was Lt. Gen. Wilhelm Bittrich, commander of the II SS Panzer Corps, who, immediately on learning of the Allied landings in the area, thought that no matter what their objective, the Arnhem and Nijmegen bridges would be involved. He immediately gave orders for his armor, the 9th and 10th SS Panzer Divisions (the armor that Field Marshal Montgomery dismissed as not being in the area), to reconnoiter and secure the areas and to hold the Arnhem and the Nijmegen bridges at all costs.

The second German officer to take steps toward establishing a defense was SS Maj. Sepp Krafft, commander of the SS Panzergrenadier Training and Reserve Battalion, who, by chance, found himself bivouacked on the edge of the British drop zones. He sounded the alarm and placed two of his companies in a defensive position between the British paratroopers and the Arnhem bridge. His third company was in reserve, bivouacked near Arnhem. He then gave orders for his outnumbered troops and armor to fight using hit-and-run tactics. Lie in ambush, strike with surprise when the British marched into them, kill and destroy, and move to a new vantage point to repeat the maneuver. He wanted to keep the British off guard, killing and crippling as many as possible while avoiding engaging them in open warfare. His goal was to delay the enemy at every step until support arrived.

Shortly after the British battalions set off on their respective missions the radios began to fail for some strange reason. Within minutes the Red Devils had lost contact with one another and the outside world. At the same time, troopers on the northern and central roads were hit by German panzers, *panzergrenadiers,* and artillery. The battle that followed was short and violent. The scouts out front were killed, others were killed and wounded, and several vehicles were destroyed. Then, as quickly as it had begun, the firing stopped and the Germans faded into the surrounding landscape.

General Urquhart, having lost all communication, became increasingly concerned. He ordered the communications officer to try to reach Major Gough but his attempts were all unsuccessful. Without communication, Urquhart was in the dark and in danger of losing control of the operation. He finally sent word by messenger that he wanted to see Major Gough in his headquarters, then nervously settled in to wait.

Meanwhile, the ambushed paratroopers reassembled and continued their trek toward the bridge, leaving their medics to care for the wounded. Hardly had they gotten underway when they were hit again with the same results. Each time the Germans would hit hard for several minutes, then they disengaged and moved back to lie in wait and hit again, and then again. The British were taking a beating but they did not falter, they pushed relentlessly on toward their assigned objectives.

The march to the bridge was supposed to take only three hours, but this battle-as-you-go march had gone beyond that point in time and they were nowhere near the bridge—and they were losing men and equipment every step of the way.

General Urquhart, not knowing where his troops were or what was happening, was not in command of his forces. His communications officer dispatched two radio jeeps to a point halfway between the landing zones and the advancing battalions in hopes of restoring communication. Still no contact. Growing increasingly worried by the minute, General Urquhart drove his jeep to the 1st Air Landing Brigade's headquarters. The radios there were also out. Urquhart was erroneously told that Major Gough had lost nearly all of his vehicles, weapons, and supplies before and during the landings and would not be able to perform his mission as planned. Due to this misinformation General Urquhart felt that he had to get in touch with his commanders to formulate and execute a new plan of attack. He again sent a messenger to find Major Gough and have him report to division headquarters.

After waiting for what must have seemed an eternity for Major Gough to show up, General Urquhart started out by jeep toward Arnhem to find Brig. Gerald Lathbury, commander of the 1st Parachute Brigade, Lieutenant Colonel Frost's attack battalion, and Major Gough's reconnaissance squadron.

Major Gough's squadron came under heavy fire from the Germans at the same time that he was informed by messenger that he was to report back to headquarters to meet with General Urquhart. Gough, following orders, turned his jeep around and left his troops to handle the skirmish themselves. The two officers were on different routes and unknowingly passed each other as they headed in opposite directions.

Confusion reigned. The Germans were attacking with a ferocity no one had expected them to be capable of. Artillery and mortar fire blanketed the approaching British, who went to ground and then scattered, some taking shelter in the wooded areas. Men were being killed and wounded and equipment was being destroyed. German tanks joined the attacks. At first some of the Brits thought the tanks were from General Horrocks's XXX Corps and had somehow beaten them to the bridge. That would have been impossible under the best of circumstances, which these clearly were not. And XXX Corps, hours behind schedule, had not yet reached its first objective, Eindhoven, nearly fifty-five miles south. The old, tired, ready-to-surrender Germans guarding the Arnhem bridge with a few ancient, worn-out tanks—which was what the Red Devils had been told by the high command they would encounter—turned out to be the battle-seasoned 9th and 10th SS Panzer Divisions and SS *panzergrenadiers,* all of whom were ready, willing, and able to fight.

Before the operation began, Maj. Brian Urquhart (no relation to General Urquhart) General Browning's young intelligence chief, tried to warn the British command, including Montgomery, that a strong German force was in the vicinity of Arnhem. He produced low-level aerial photos of panzers sitting virtually *on* the intended drop zones prior to the drop, as well as information reported by the Dutch Underground on the German armor and troop buildup in the area and their willing and able fighting capabilities. The young major was rebuffed, hushed, and then sent home on furlough "to recover from a nervous condition." His photos and other intelligence information that suggested disaster awaited the British at Arnhem were trashed and not mentioned in any of the command briefings. This thrust to end the war would take place.

Lieutenant Colonel Dobie's 1st Battalion, marching east on the northern route, ran head-on into the 9th SS Panzer Division. He was forced to alter his course to the south and attempt to join up with Lieutenant Colonel Frost's 2d Battalion for a combined attack on the bridge. Meanwhile, Major Gough had arrived back at headquarters, where he learned that General Urquhart had left to go looking for him and Brigadier Lathbury. Major Gough left immediately, heading back from whence he had come.

General Urquhart traveled the Utrecht–Arnhem highway a short way, then turned south on a side road to the river road on which Frost's battalion was moving. Turning east he ran into Frost's trailing Headquarters Company and relayed to them the misinformation about Major Gough's disaster. He told them they would have to make the attack on the bridge without Major Gough's troops, and then left to look for Brigadier Lathbury.

Retracing his route west, then north, he came to the center road and again turned east. A short distance later he found Brigadier Lathbury with Lt. Col. J. A. C. Fitch's 3d Battalion, which was under heavy mortar and artillery attack. Lathbury and Urquhart took cover in slit trenches while they made plans to correct the situation. Lieutenant Colonel Fitch's troops were engaged in a hard-fought battle with Waffen SS troops, half-tracks, tanks, and artillery. It was tough, but by sheer courage and determination the British paratroopers pressed their attack forward.

Meanwhile, Lieutenant Colonel Frost's men reached the railroad bridge—their first objective. They advanced toward it sending one platoon ahead on a dead run. The paratroopers reached the bridge and were running toward the far end when the Germans detonated preset charges, completely destroying a span near the south end. The bridge was useless. It was a little after 6 P.M.

Sensing an urgent need for speed, the battalion raced on to its second objective, the pontoon bridge that lay about a mile west of the main Arnhem bridge. So far they had engaged in only hit-and-run small-arms battles—nothing like what was being experienced by the paratroopers fighting in the north against the Waffen SS panzers and SS *panzergrenadiers.*

It was as though the Germans, in their protective concern over the main roads, had forgotten this secondary road that ran alongside the meandering Neder Rijn. It was just getting dark when Frost's men arrived at the pontoon bridge site. Even in the growing darkness they could see that the bridge's center span was missing. The Germans had removed and hidden it elsewhere. Strike two. One more strike and they would be out. It was up to them to seize the Arnhem bridge intact.

Night had fallen by the time 3d Battalion arrived at the outskirts of Oosterbeek with General Urquhart and Brigadier Lathbury. It had become too confusing and dangerous to advance any farther, so a halt was called and the men dug in while the generals occupied a large house overlooking the road.

The following morning all hell broke loose again. The Germans had infiltrated all during the night and now held positions of strength all around them. They opened up with rifles and automatic weapons fire. Snipers in attics, windows, and other places of advantage opened fire. Mortars and rocket-propelled mortars slammed in. Artillery opened up, blanketing the paratroopers with explosions laced with hot, ragged steel. The paratroopers' ranks fragmented. Men ran to take cover wherever they could find it. Many were killed or wounded. General Urquhart and Brigadier Lathbury hurriedly made their way to houses on the side streets. They took refuge in one of the houses there and, by the time the battle got into full swing, German soldiers had infested the area. The two top-ranking officers in the division were trapped behind enemy lines with little hope of escape.

Frost's troopers, traveling along the river road, finally reached the Arnhem bridge after seven hours of hit-and-run battles. The bridge seemed deserted and undefended except for two pillboxes, one at each end. When the paratroopers moved onto the bridge and headed for the south end all hell broke loose as hidden Germans opened up with small arms as soon as the pillboxes began firing. The Brits rushed forward through a heavy cross fire. They brought forward flamethrowers and bathed the pillboxes in flame while Piat gunners fired shaped-charge missiles against the emplacements. There were loud explosions and fire engulfed the pillboxes. German soldiers ran screaming onto the bridge completely aflame. The pillboxes were silenced, but the Brits could not advance past that point because of the flames and the burning and exploding ammo stored inside as well as the intense small-arms firing coming in from the south end of the bridge. They had to fall back on the entrance ramp and take positions in nearby buildings. Battle lines were being naturally set between the north and south ends of the bridge with no-man's-land in between. The real war had begun.

Although it had taken more than twice the expected time to reach the bridge, Frost was confident General Horrocks would arrive on schedule and that he and his men could hold until the main airborne force fighting its way from the drop zones arrived.

Frost's men made two more attempts to reach the south end of the bridge but they were driven back by heavy small-arms fire and machine-gun fire from an armored half-track at that end. As time went by, the Germans strengthened their hold on the south end. Unknown to Frost and his battalion, there was a ferry that carried cars, trucks, and people between Heveadorp on the north side of the Neder Rijn to Driel on the south bank and back. Half the airborne troops could have been ferried across to make a coordinated attack from both ends of the bridge at the same time. A classic West Point maneuver that almost never presents itself in reality was allowed to slip away. The existence of this ferry and the assignment for its capture were never mentioned in the briefings. The high command detailing the master plan had completely overlooked it. Frost and his troops had unknowingly walked right past it on their march from the DZ to the bridge.

The British overlooked two other factors that might have changed the fortunes of war. Dutch resistance fighters had offered their services, knowledge, and lives to the Brits but were turned down. Perhaps it was because the paratroopers were self-reliant and simply didn't know who they could trust. Whatever the reason, they chose to follow orders and go it alone. Because of this they were unaware of the Underground telephone service used by the resistance fighters. When their radios went blank right after their arrival the British, had they known, could have picked up the closest civilian phone and called over secret lines to anywhere from Arnhem to Eindhoven and beyond.

The Americans used the resistance fighters to help destroy the Germans in Eindhoven, and they took advantage of the Underground phone system from the first day on at Zon to contact Allied forces from Zon to Eindhoven and Nijmegen.

The battle lines had been drawn. German Waffen SS *panzergrenadiers* held the south end of the bridge and the British held the north end, with the 9th and 10th SS Panzer Divisions surrounding and dividing the British battalions in the north and throughout Arnhem, like a gigantic sandwich with the British in the middle. The only hope for these troops lay in the fact that more paratroopers would be arriving to beef them up and together hold out until the arrival of General Horrocks and his XXX Corps within the next forty-eight hours or so.

During that first night the Germans began sending in wave after wave of SS *panzergrenadiers,* infantry, and whatever other men they could muster. Work crews, office personnel, and anyone else available were armed on the spot and ordered to attack the English positions. All available troops were sent forward under the cover of darkness to infiltrate the houses held by the English in Arnhem. Street by street, house by house, and room by room the battles raged in bitter face-to-face, hand-to-hand combat. Bayonet charges by the English were common. They would drive the Germans out of houses and into the streets with bayonets and knives, then return to their strongholds, only to have the equally stubborn enemy return to attack again and again.

Unarmed Dutch civilians helped in the only way they could. Knowing the Germans were massing armor for a drive against the troopers, the Dutch dragged the bodies of Englishmen, Germans, and civilians and stacked them up to form dikes across the roads in hopes the Germans would not drive their tanks through them to get at the English. It was a brutal night of close-in, hand-to-hand fighting. The wounded were dragged into cellars and the dead left where they fell, to be stacked with the others forming the roadblocks. Troopers and civilians alike slipped in greasy puddles of human blood as they went about their chores of killing, defending, and surviving.

So ended the first night. Part of the British force was dug in on the drop zones. Other troopers were attempting to keep the routes open from the DZs to the bridge, and still others were fighting to reach the men holding the north end of the bridge. The men holding in place on the bridge, knowing their forces were fragmented, their commander missing, their communications out, and running low on ammo and troops, vowed to hold to the last man. None gave up hope that General Horrocks would arrive with his massive armored force and take the war into Germany.

September 18, 1944, D plus 1. The Dutch resistance telephoned a message via their Underground line to the headquarters of General Gavin, commander of the 82d Airborne Division near Nijmegen, that the Germans had brought in armor. The British were losing the battle for Arnhem and the bridge. It was the first news the Allies had about the Red Devils, and it most certainly did not look good. The message was relayed back down the ladder to Eindhoven in hopes of spurring the British XXX Corps on.

On D day a Waco glider crashed on its LZ, killing all the occupants on impact. A German soldier rummaging through the wreckage found a briefcase containing a complete set of maps and the order detailing the units involved, their missions, code words and names, dates, times, and places of succeeding drops. The briefcase was turned over to Col. Gen. Kurt Student, who in turn passed it along to Field Marshal Walter Model. Now the whole plan in complete detail lay bare before the enemy, even before the incoming troops had completed their landings. But the plan and papers were too good, too detailed. Field Marshal Model had his staff examine them. They agreed that the plans were too complete, too informative, too convenient, too good to be true. Model decided the plans must have been planted by the Allies. It would take time to determine if they were indeed what they seemed to be. If they proved to be the real thing, proper action would then be taken.

Early in the morning on the second day a German armored patrol returning from a reconnaissance mission that had taken it from north of Arnhem to south of Nijmegen left several armored vehicles at the south end of the Nijmegen bridge to hold against possible attack. The patrol continued north, leaving more armored vehicles near Elst, halfway between Nijmegen and Arnhem, where they could make a run to either bridge in case of need. The patrol then continued back toward the Arnhem bridge with orders to clear it of enemy troops reportedly holding the north end.

The German armor arrived at the Arnhem bridge at 9:30 A.M. and charged at full speed across the bridge to smash the British lines. At first the British again thought that it was General Horrocks's armor coming to relieve them, then they realized that it was Germans bearing down on them. With machine guns blazing, the first German vehicles smashed their way through the lightly armed paratroopers. A larger German armor and infantry force followed.

The British opened up on the main force with a barrage of small-arms fire and hand grenades. Some of the half-track drivers were killed and their out-of-control vehicles slammed into one another. Others, racing in from the rear, smashed into the stalled ones or speeded up in an attempt to smash through the ruined armor and plunged over the side of the ramp to crash in a pile of twisted steel and mangled bodies a hundred feet below. The British paratroopers fired into the mass of German soldiers following the armor. Caught in a murderous cross fire, they died on the spot.

Firing from both sides increased and ricocheting tracers entered nearby houses, setting them afire. The flames quickly spread to other buildings. Men on both sides died or were wounded as the battle's intensity increased amid more crashing armor, bodies, and burning buildings. Twelve German armored vehicles were wrecked. The ones that were able withdrew to the south end of the bridge to take refuge out of sight of the British defenders.

The Red Devils of the 1st Airborne Division had fought with guts and small arms against an all-out enemy armor attack and held. Their confidence was strengthened by the knowledge that the second lift would be coming in that day and would soon be followed by the arrival of the British armor. Then the tables would turn. The paratroopers never lost faith. In fact, their faith grew in light of their victory over enemy armor with small arms. Imagine what they could have accomplished with proper weapons and a full complement of troops.

Unknown to them, General Horrocks had bivouacked his column of armor five miles south of Eindhoven the night of the seventeenth. General Horrocks's convoy was confined to a one-tank front on a narrow road bordered by fields that would not support heavy tanks. Battles had taken place every foot of the way against German self-propelled guns, tanks, and infantry. At times they were stalled by a well-entrenched enemy while awaiting strikes by rocket-firing Typhoon fighter-bombers called in to open the way. There were also problems moving through mobs of cheering Dutch civilians. By then the British armor was thirty-six hours behind schedule.

That wasn't the only delay, however. The second lift scheduled to drop into the Arnhem area with troop reinforcements, ammo, food, medical supplies, artillery, and vehicles was sitting on airfields back in England. They were fogged in; no one could take off.

Finally the fog cleared and the lift started. Sterling bombers and C-47s loaded with paratroopers took off from airfields all over England. Many more were towing Waco, Horsa, and Hamilcar gliders loaded with troops, artillery, jeeps, and ammunition for artillery, mortars, and small-caliber weapons. The air trains heading for Holland were even larger and longer than the ones that set out on D day. The troops on board felt they had it made. The paratroopers who had dropped the day before would have the few old tired Germans bottled up in prisoner of war cages by this time, the bridges secured, and the DZs and LZs would be a parade ground picnic. In fact, one trooper carried a football under his jacket so they could play a game on the DZ before heading on to their assigned objectives.

In the meantime, the Germans, believing the captured plans in the briefcase just might be for real, called in fighters from other combat areas to patrol around Arnhem at the time the drop was scheduled to take place. By the time the fog cleared and the lift came in, most of the German fighters had been recalled to their bases or were on the ground refueling. Still, many did get back into the air and they attacked with a vengeance. Fortunately, none got through to fire at the troopships. The Allied fighters flying escort destroyed them or drove them off. However, the enemy antiaircraft, which was heavily bolstered, did wreak terrible damage and destruction on the flight. Many ships were destroyed or damaged in the air, resulting in heavy losses of men, equipment, and aircraft.

The British airborne troops coming in by parachute and glider found their DZs and LZs were a battlefield, not a parade ground. The paratroopers who had landed the day before were fighting for their very lives trying to hold the drop zones against Germans attacking with infantry, armored vehicles, artillery, and mortars. Men hitting the DZ were killed by machine guns cross firing over the field, by rifle fire, and by mortar bursts. Troopers were killed or wounded as they released their harnesses or attempted to open the gliders to retrieve the equipment they had brought in. It was an all-out struggle just to get off the field. It was certainly no place or time for a football game.

Of eighty tons of equipment dropped by air, only twelve tons were dropped where the Brits could gather them in. The rest went to the

Germans. Several British artillerymen landed on the south side of the Neder Rijn with their field piece. Finding the ferry still operational, they loaded the gun on board and made it across to the north bank.

It was suggested very strongly to British officers by a former Dutch army officer that they take control of the ferry, place their artillery on the Westerbouwing, the only high ground around, and thereby control the ferry crossing. They would then be able to roam back and forth at will between the north and south banks of the Neder Rijn with their troops, equipment, and tanks. The ferry could support three tanks at a time. Again the English refused the advice of the Dutch, saying they would follow orders and do it their way.

The arriving British troops formed up on the DZs and LZs and made their way down German-infiltrated streets toward the city of Arnhem, fighting every step of the way. In the meantime, the Germans began moving tanks and other armored vehicles from the 9th and 10th SS Panzer Divisions toward the bridge after successfully cutting off the reinforcing troops from the troops holding the north end of the bridge. The British on the roads into Arnhem and holding the north end of the bridge were fighting as individual groups out of physical and radio contact with one another.

Late in the night on the eighteenth the Germans moved a force of fifty armored vehicles, including Tiger tanks, half-tracks, and *panzergrenadiers* toward the bridge in Arnhem. Several of the tanks broke off and headed toward Oosterbeek. The Dutch Underground relayed this information by telephone to a disbelieving British command in Ooosterbeek. Only after the message was confirmed by a Dutch liaison officer did the British believe it.

Meanwhile, Frost's men holding the bridge were being pounded mercilessly by heavy artillery, mortar, and small-arms fire. This beating had been going on since the panzer unit had arrived at the south end of the bridge. All the while his men were being killed and wounded without count. Their ammo was low, their food was all but gone, and the troopers were using whatever cloth could be found in the houses to stem the blood from their wounds. Then the Germans shut off the water to the area and began bringing up flamethrowers and *panzerfausts* in an all-out attempt to burn and blast them out. Still the British would not bow. They dug in deeper, fortifying one another with the reminder that Horrocks was on the way with armor and troops and should be in Arnhem within a matter of hours. They could certainly hold till then.

More enemy armor was moving into the city, building in strength. German tanks and *panzergrenadiers* infiltrated the side streets everywhere, working themselves and their self-propelled guns, tanks, and heavy weapons in between the British battalions attempting to advance to the bridge and Frost's positions, further isolating the individual groups of paratroopers and with each attack reducing their numbers. Undaunted, the Red Devils attacked and counterattacked, at times regaining lost ground and streets.

It was in one of these attacks that General Urquhart's hiding place was overrun by his own troops. Freed, he made his way back to resume his command in Oosterbeek. Brigadier Lathbury had been wounded and removed to a shelter to be cared for by medics. On his return, Urquhart was received as one risen from the dead. He had been missing for thirty-nine hours.

September 19, 1944, D plus 2. Horrocks's lead armor finally reached Grave, where it linked up with troopers from the 82d Airborne Division at 8:30 A.M. The huge column of armor, trucks, artillery, and men then moved slowly northward, reaching Nijmegen around noon.

We troopers of the 101st Airborne Division were proud. It had cost us the lives and wounding and crippling of many of our comrades, but we had taken the highway and bridges from Eindhoven through Zon and on to Veghel from an overwhelming enemy force and laid down the royal carpet over which the British columns now rolled. Our comrades in the 82d Airborne had done the same thing in their sector, taking and securing the bridges and the road from Grave to Nijmegen. We had accomplished our mission ahead of schedule. Together we had taken and held the road to Arnhem.

General Horrocks and Maj. Gen. Allan Adair, commander of the Guards Armoured Division, were brought up to the front from the rear of the long column to meet with the 82d's commander, General Gavin. The British generals were shocked to learn that the Nijmegen bridge hadn't already been taken and that they couldn't just simply roll on over on the way to Arnhem. This was the first time they realized just how hard pressed the Americans had been to keep the drop zones and the road to Arnhem open and out of German hands.

General Gavin laid out his plan to use his troops to attack the bridge from both ends with the aid of British tanks on the south end. The bridge needed taking now, and the paratroopers just didn't have the kind of firepower the British had. The British generals were shocked by Gavin's plan: an assault river crossing by paratroopers! He intended to send one of his battalions across the river downstream in small boats to attack the strong fortifications and dug-in enemy on the north end of the railroad and main road bridges. At the same time, another battalion would attack from the south backed by British tanks firing into the enemy positions across the river on the north end of the bridge.

In time the assault boats were brought forward and moved to the proper spot for launch. Paratroopers attacked the bridge from the south with tanks providing supporting fire. At the same time, the men downstream paddled their flimsy craft for the opposite shore while the Germans fired on them from the north shore with everything from rifles and machine guns to antiaircraft guns, mortars, and cannon. Many men were killed in midstream by this fire while others drowned after falling from capsized boats, their bodies swept away in the current. But the assault force made it across and charged across yards of open shoreline through withering fire with a vengeance after seeing their comrades murdered while helpless on the open water without cover or concealment. Many Germans were not given a chance to surrender. At the end of a very bloody fight the 82d's paratroopers raised an American flag on the north end of the main bridge, which was safely in American hands except for a few diehards holding out in the middle with small arms, machine guns, mortars, and an 88mm cannon.

Seeing the American flag waving on the other end of the bridge, the British rushed several tanks over, firing their machine guns without letup. They herded the subdued Germans off the bridge to the north end, where they were taken prisoner. The Germans had tried to blow the bridge while the British tanks were on it but the charges failed to go off. All wires and fuses were then searched out and cut and the explosives neutralized. The attack began at 3 P.M. and was all over at 7:15. Both the railroad and the main road bridges at Nijmegen were securely in Allied hands.

The British tanks that made the crossing came to a halt and formed a defensive line on the northern approach. Colonel Reuben H. Tucker, commander of the 82d's 504th PIR, goaded them to go on.

"It's only eleven miles to Arnhem!" he shouted. "Go on! Get to Arnhem. We've got paratroopers there waiting on us."

But the tanks just sat there. There was no rush to get to Arnhem, only eleven miles away. The tankers said their orders were to stay until their infantry could be brought up to the front, possibly the next day. Then they would attack together, not until then.

The Americans were furious. If infantry were needed for the attack, why weren't they there following the tanks across the bridge? Paratroopers belong to a deep-rooted brotherhood. They all know what it is to jump behind enemy lines and rely on ground troops and tanks to break through in a very limited timeframe to relieve them. Every minute counted.

The 82d troopers couldn't believe the British tankers would just sit there and leave the Red Devils to their fate. Patton would have charged full speed over that bridge without hesitating and then raced hell bent to and over that damned bridge at Arnhem—with or without infantry. He once told his tankers when they complained about having no fuel for their tanks: "Then get out and walk, but keep going forward."

The few British tanks on the north end of the Nijmegen bridge stayed in place, not moving. The large body of tanks at the south end also sat there. American paratroopers burned with a fury that still smolders to this day. They had lost 134 men killed, wounded, or missing taking that bridge so XXX Corps could get to the Red Devils still hanging on in Arnhem, and the English stopped to brew compo tea.

September 20, 1944, D plus 3. General Sosabowski's brigade was finally going to make its jump on the south side of the Neder Rijn near Elden. Their jump the day before had been called off after he and his men had boarded the planes ready to go. Now, with all his troops aboard the air train, his plane led the way to the takeoff point, then stopped and waited. An officer came aboard and informed Sosabowski that his jump had been postponed for another twenty-four hours. Sosabowski and his troopers were angry beyond description.

The Germans, meanwhile, had been bringing tanks up all during the night. Once in place, they opened up on the British strongholds, blasting the walls down cannon shot by cannon shot, brick by brick. Fires broke out but still the Red Devils refused to surrender. Basements around the northern end of the Arnhem bridge filled with wounded. Without food or water and down to their last few rounds, they continued to defy and taunt the enemy. Lieutenant Colonel Frost was wounded and carried to a basement. The building was burning down over them, near collapse. Finally, in the name of humanity and out of compassion for his wounded, Frost gave the order for the wounded to surrender and for those who were still able to get around to try to make it back to division headquarters and fight on with General Urquhart.

After contact was made with the enemy, they moved in to finally take by agreement what they couldn't take by arms. German soldiers carried the wounded British from the burning buildings, which collapsed into the basements a short time later. The German soldiers, many of whom were veterans of the Russian front moved, not with hatred, but in awe and admiration, among the wounded British, giving them food, water, rum, and chocolate, complimenting them on being the toughest warriors they had ever come up against. Never had these Germans, veterans of European and Russian battlefields, fought against anyone as fearless and tough as the Red Devils of the British 1st Airborne Division. Those paratroopers rank among the most courageous, tenacious fighters to ever enter the field of mortal combat. There was no shame in their surrender, only well earned, undying pride mixed with the bitter knowledge that they were expendable, their lives spent like pennies. It was over. Horrocks and his tanks never arrived. They had been thrown away.

September 21, 1944, D plus 4. General Sosabowski's drop zone had been changed from Elden to Driel, still on the south side of the

Neder Rijn. His orders now called for his brigade to capture the ferry and get over to the north bank to reinforce General Urquhart's troops and hold a bridgehead on that side until XXX Corps arrived. They would then retake the Arnhem bridge and go on with Operation Market-Garden as planned.

Sosabowski's flight took off this time but soon flew into increasingly bad weather. Nearly half of his aircraft had to abort and turn back. Some planes and gliders were lost en route. Then the Poles ran into another kind of storm, a storm of enemy fighters that attacked with a fury, destroying many planes and gliders before they reached the DZ. When they finally jumped, General Sosabowski's troopers descended into an inferno on a battlefield that was their newly assigned drop zone. With the captured Market-Garden plans in hand, the Germans were able to bring in fighter planes, antiaircraft guns, ground troops, and artillery to completely ring the DZ. The German infantry set up machine guns and mortars and lay in wait for the Poles. It is a miracle that any of them survived the drop at all.

After ridding themselves of their harness and grabbing their weapons and packs they found what cover they could in shallow ditches and alongside the dikes. Many were killed getting out of their harness and while retrieving their gear. After forming up in small groups they fought their way off the DZs and prepared to move out to their objectives.

Sosabowski's DZs for the heavy equipment on the north side of the river had been guarded by the Brits. However, the Germans knew the locations and attacked with overwhelming forces, driving the British off and shooting down a goodly number of resupply aircraft as they passed overhead. They then gathered in what equipment and supplies the transports managed to drop on the captured fields. Sosabowski and his men were in serious trouble.

The Poles made their way by guts, fighting, and luck to the ferry site only to find that the boat was gone, nowhere in sight. Although some believed that the Germans had sunk it, it was found downstream several days later, where it had run aground and lodged after breaking loose in a high wind during a fierce rainstorm. The Poles found several small boats and with grim determination managed to secure a line to both banks of the river. They then spent the night ferrying men across the river four and five at a time, pulling the small boats back each time using the attached line.

German troops discovered them during the night and trained machine guns on their positions, firing all through the night. Most of the Poles made it across but many were either wounded or killed by machine-gun fire.

The British were in the same fix on their own drop zones. They were shelled, mortared, machine-gunned, and assaulted by tanks and infantry. Much of the fighting was hand to hand. The Germans also moved antiaircraft batteries into strategic places to cripple and shoot down a number of Allied planes. They then gathered in the equipment that was meant for the British, who were still without ammo, medical supplies, food, and the chocolate and rum that the Germans were now enjoying. The men of the 1st Airborne Division were suffering in ways that no human should have to suffer. Yet still they fought on.

The last resupply drop was made on September 23. It was also met by an overpowering enemy force that all but wiped out the troopers and took away their supplies.

In these last days the Germans, ordered to finish off the British once and for all, mounted an all-out drive with armor, infantry, and artillery that blasted, mortared, and shot everything in front of and around them in a holocaust of death and destruction. Tanks wheeled, churned, and fired indiscriminately into first aid stations as well as into fortified positions and foxholes. Many times during the hand-to-hand struggles troops became so entangled that German and British soldiers would leap into the same foxhole or slit trench.

Still the Red Devils and the supporting Polish troops held.

In the end, General Urquhart was informed that he could expect no help from Horrocks. He and his men would have to make their own way to the banks of the Neder Rijn, where an assortment of boats would attempt to ferry across what survivors they could before sunup. It would be a one-shot deal. Anyone not making it was on his own from that point on. The wounded would have to be left to the Germans.

The evacuation began at 9 P.M. and was covered by a massive artillery barrage on German positions by the British on the south shore of the river. Assault boats and an array of whatever other small boats could be found, including a DUKW amphibious truck, came across, loaded up with survivors, and made their way back. Some boats were so overloaded that they sank. Men either swam or drowned. Halfway through the evacuation the operation was discovered by the Germans, who immediately set up and began cutting into them with small-arms, mortar, and artillery fire, sending up parachute flares all the while.

By sunrise it was all over. Many men were naked, having shed their clothes and boots in order to swim the four hundred yards to safety through a swift current in the dark. British troops and Dutch civilians were on hand to meet them, giving what clothing they had to cover and keep the survivors warm. They then hustled them off to where they were given hot tea and biscuits.

The Red Devils of the 1st Airborne Division and their Polish counterparts had been left to their fate in Arnhem by a toddling, hundred-mile-long, overstuffed convoy. General Urquhart's and Sosabowski's commands had gone in with a combined total of 10,005 troopers. Only 2,163 Red Devils, 160 Poles, and 75 downed Allied airmen and members of the Dutch resistance—a total of 2,398—returned. The division suffered 1,200 dead and 6,482 wounded, missing, or captured, for a total of 7,682 casualties.

The Red Devils of the 1st Airborne Division had fought one of the toughest battles in recorded history. Each man was a hero.

Thousands of Americans, British, Poles, and Dutch, paid the ultimate price for freedom in Holland. In return they received a road that ended nowhere.

Afterword

We may fail to realize it at the time that perhaps the powers that be attempt to forewarn us of the future. If only we knew, we may well prepare ourselves. But I have learned that even though we are told the facts straight forward, it is human to reject that which we do not wish to accept.

We, the 101st, the 82d, and the British 6th Airborne Divisions parachuted into Normandy on June 6, 1944, at 1:14 A.M. to lead the Allies into breaching the walls of "Festung Europa," Hitler's "impenetrable" fortress. Our actions there were impressive enough to cause Gen. Dwight D. Eisenhower to form the First Allied Airborne Army (The First Triple A). The American 101st, the 82d, and the 17th Airborne Divisions, along with the British 1st and 6th Airborne Divisions and the Polish 1st Brigade were banded together as members of that airborne army.

On September 17, 1944, the 101st, the 82d, and the British 1st Brigade parachuted and glider-landed into the Netherlands as members of that army and fought well, accomplishing all assigned missions ahead of schedule, suffering heavy casualties in the process. The American 101st and 82d Divisions were all but decimated under Field Marshal Bernard L. Montgomery's command there. The British 1st Airborne Division and the Polish 1st Brigade were destroyed as fighting units under that same command.

They had been surrounded by superior armor and armor grenadier forces, run over by panzer divisions, pounded mercilessly by heavy and close-range artillery, and attacked frontally on all sides by numerically superior infantry and SS forces until they were beaten into the ground. The British Airborne never gave up; they never surrendered. The few remaining survivors, ragged and torn, fought their way out of the encirclement when they were finally ordered to withdraw. The world, even the enemy, paid homage to the bravery of these unbeatable soldiers. But there was a loss, and losses do not win wars.

We fought in that same campaign, but being separated by the wide German holy Rijn River were unable to go to the aid of our allies. We could only wait in anguish on the south bank as our airborne brothers in arms were destroyed slowly on the north. They had held for eight battle-filled days and nights, retired from battle only when ordered to do so.

We had been party to the events and held ringside seats to witness British and German history in the battle for Arnhem. Little did we know then that within weeks the 101st Airborne Division would mirror that same situation in battle for the small Belgian city of Bastogne, the key to the now historic Battle of the Bulge. The powers that be had allowed us to preview that which they had in store for us. The panzer divisions, the panzer grenadiers, the heavy artillery, all to surround us in an attempt to destroy us once and forever.

In being surrounded, the British had held in Arnhem against insurmountable odds for eight days and nights of bitter all-out battle before being ordered to withdraw. Our division was to hold in Bastogne against nine panzer armor and armor grenadier divisions in bitter all-out battles for eight days and nights before Patton's 4th Armored Division broke through enemy lines to reinforce our paratroops and drive the enemy back to where they came from.

Of course there was no wide German holy Rijn River to impede Patton's force from driving through to meet up with us, but there was a surrounding river of thirty-eight German armor and armored infantry divisions to cross. Our defense of Bastogne held; we were reinforced and our counterattack was accomplished, which ended in victory for the Allies. The German troop tanks, vehicles, and supplies expended in this last great German offensive thrust had so drained the enemy that their total unconditional defeat was sealed in World War II.

Even so, the enemy fought tenaciously until the last shot was fired. Until that last shot we fought on through Alsace, the Rhineland, Bavaria, and Austria. It cost lives and took many battles to finally kill a dying Nazi Germany.